The Way Computer Graphics Works

The Way Computer Graphics Works

Olin Lathrop

WILEY COMPUTER PUBLISHING

John Wiley & Sons, Inc.
New York • Chichester • Weinheim • Brisbane • Singapore • Toronto

Executive Publisher: Katherine Schowalter
Senior Editor: Marjorie Spencer
Associate Managing Editor: Angela Murphy
Text Design & Composition: North Market Street Graphics

Library of Congress Cataloging-in-Publication Data:
Lathrop, Olin.
    The way computer graphics works / Olin Lathrop.
        p.   cm.
    "Wiley Computer Publishing."
    Includes bibliographical references and index.
    ISBN: 0-471-13040-0 (paper : alk. paper)
    1. Computer graphics.   I. Title.
  T385.L382   1997
  006.6—dc20   96-42688

Printed in the United States of America
10 9 8 7 6 5 4 3 2 1

Is This Book for You?

Hi. Because you're reading this, I'll assume you've got at least some curiosity about computer graphics. If you're simply looking for the solution to a particular problem or want to learn how to run a particular application, this book isn't for you. If, however, you want to *understand* something about the technology, then read on.

This is a good "first" book on computer graphics. It provides a context for understanding future information and will give you considerable insight into what goes on behind the scenes. We'll stick to the technology of computer graphics, and we won't talk about particular applications, systems, or the standard of the week. Think of it this way: You don't really need to know how an engine works to just drive a car, but it's useful in getting good mileage and performance without doing any damage. It's also the first step in becoming a backyard mechanic or tinkerer. Fortunately, computer graphics won't leave you covered with grease and smelling like a fire hazard.

I've tried to make this book unintimidating and approachable. Understanding the basics of computer graphics doesn't require advanced knowledge in math, physics, or computers, so there's no need to present it that way. As you've probably noticed by now, the style of this book is "me" talking to "you." Not only do I think it's easier for you to read, but it's also what comes naturally for me to write.

As you flip through the rest of this book to decide whether it's right for you, I hope you'll notice that I've tried to explain things with pictures instead of with equations.

After all, graphics is ultimately for communicating. It's always amazed me how other graphics books don't apply what they're talking about. Full-color illustrations scattered throughout the book do make it more expensive to produce, but both the publisher and I thought you'd appreciate the difference.

Acknowledgments

Although only my name and the publisher's appear on the cover, a number of other people deserve recognition for their substantial assistance in the creation of this book.

IMAGES

The following people provided or helped me obtain images for some of the illustrations:

Professor **Norman Badler**, Director of the Center for Human Modeling and Simulation, Computer and Information Science Department, University of Pennsylvania in Philadelphia.

Jules Bloomenthal of Microsoft in Redmond, Washington.

Brian DeRosa of Westford Academy, class of 1997. (Westford Academy is the public high school in Westford, Massachusetts.)

Bruce Edwards of Octree Corporation in Cupertino, California.

Eric Haines of 3D/EYE in Ithaca, New York.

Mike Hollick of the University of Pennsylvania in Philadelphia.

Eric Nelson of Hewlett-Packard in Fort Collins, Colorado.

Justin Ryan of Westford Academy, class of 1996.

Kay Seirup of Pixar in Richmond, California.

Alvy Ray Smith of Microsoft in Redmond, Washington.

Nathaniel Wieselquist of Westford Academy, class of 1996.

Professor **Brian Wyvill** of the computer science department, University of Calgary in Calgary, Alberta.

REVIEW

The following people were very helpful in reviewing early versions of the manuscript and making useful suggestions.

Brian DeRosa of Westford Academy, class of 1997.

Connie Farb of AVS in Waltham, Massachusetts.

Micah Shaw of Westford Academy, class of 1998.

Contents

1

Mandatory Basics

This chapter introduces a few very basic items you need to understand to make sense of just about everything else.

IMAGES AND PIXELS

In modern computer graphics, an **image** is solely a rectangular grid, or array, of **pixels**. The word *pixel* supposedly stands for *picture element*. (No, I don't know where the X came from either.) The pixels in an image are themselves little rectangles, all the same size and shape. Each pixel is *one* solid color throughout, *by definition.*

It's important to remember that a pixel is the logical picture element inside the computer. Some image-output hardware may use many little color dots to display an image. These color dots are not necessarily the same things as pixels. We'll get into this more, especially when talking about color cathode-ray tubes on page 10. The **resolution** of an image refers to how closely packed the pixels are when displayed. For example, there may be 37 pixels per millimeter on a computer monitor, or 300 pixels per inch on a color printer. It therefore doesn't make much sense to talk about the resolution of an image inside the computer because the pixels there don't have a physical size.

The right image of Figure 1.1 is blown up so that you can clearly see the pixels. See how each pixel is a little rectangle that's always the same color throughout? That means there's no such thing as a smooth curve in a computer image. The illusion of smooth curves is achieved mostly by using large quantities of pixels, and sometimes a little cleverness. We'll talk about some of this cleverness, called antialiasing, on page 139.

Colors and Color Spaces

If I asked you what color your car is, you might reply "blue." But what if I am color blind? How would you describe the color blue itself? We all (at least those of us who can see colors) seem to agree on which colors are which, but how do we *describe* a color?

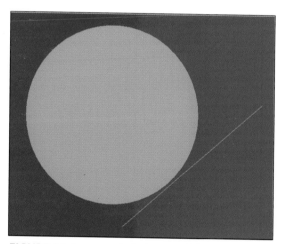 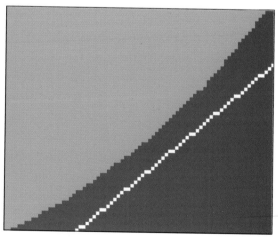

FIGURE 1.1 Image and pixels example.
Images are just rectangular grids of pixels. The pixels are clearly visible in the blowup on the right. Note that this means there are no truly curved shapes in a computer image. The illusion of smooth curves is achieved only by using lots and lots of pixels.

Computers can't perceive colors the way we do, so we have to find a way to describe them. We do this by describing the light itself. It turns out that due to how our eyes work, three independent values, or three degrees of freedom, are required to specify a color. This means colors are stored in the computer as three independent numbers. However, there can be many different schemes for exactly what the three numbers mean. Each of these different schemes is called a **color space**.

Let's look at an example with two degrees of freedom (two independent values), one that has nothing to do with colors. Suppose I am a pirate, and I need to note where I've buried my treasure on a small island. I could start on the tallest hill and record exactly how far I had to go east, then north. Or I could start at the same hill, but instead record the angle from north and the direct distance. Both these schemes result in two independent numbers, but the meaning of the numbers is quite different in each scheme.

Just as you can come up with many different ways to describe where the treasure is buried, people have come up with many different color spaces. Now we'll talk about the most common ones in computer graphics.

Red, Green, Blue (RGB) Color Space   Just about all computer graphics hardware and software use the red, green, blue (RGB) color space, at least internally. A color is described as separate red, green, and blue components. Each component can vary from 0 to 1, meaning black to maximum brightness, or intensity. Therefore, the RGB color $(0, 0, 0)$ is black, and $(1, 1, 1)$ is the brightest possible white. Yellow results in the combination of red and green, so $(1, 1, 0)$ is bright yellow. Half-intensity yellow, which looks brownish, is $(.5, .5, 0)$.

Figure 1.2 shows the RGB color cube. This is what you get by mapping the separate red, green, and blue components to the coordinate axes. Can you figure out the color at the hidden cube corner? See the figure caption for the answer.

Intensity, Hue, Saturation Color Space   Another common color space uses three numbers called *intensity, hue,* and *saturation.* This approach is closer to the way people think about colors. Usually, this kind of color space is found in the user interface. The user interacts with the program using intensity, hue, and saturation, which are then converted to RGB for internal use.

What are these intensity, hue, and saturation values? Intensity is simply how light or dark the color is. Hue describes whether the color is red, blue, Hawaiian coral pink,

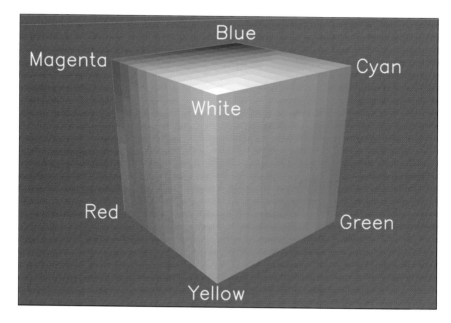

FIGURE 1.2 The red, green, blue (RGB) color cube.
The red, green, and blue color components have been mapped to coordinate axes. The color at the hidden cube corner is black.

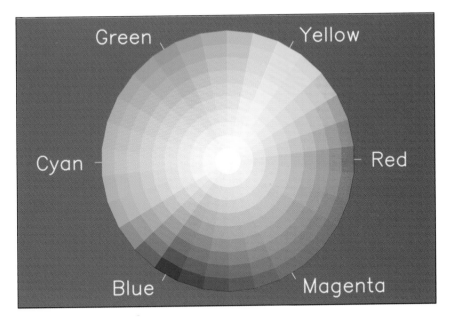

FIGURE 1.3
Hue/saturation color
wheel.
Hue varies around the
circle, while saturation is
zero in the center and
maximum at the
outside. Intensity is
maximum everywhere.

morning-sunset orange, or whatever. Saturation is the color's boldness or vividness. Pale or washed-out colors have a low saturation. A saturation of 0 means you have a shade of gray. Fire-engine red has a high saturation, whereas pink is a low-saturation red.

Figure 1.3 shows different combinations of hue and saturation at the maximum possible intensity. This kind of diagram is often called a **color wheel**. Notice that hue doesn't have a minimum or maximum value, but goes around in an endless loop. The exact encoding of the intensity, hue, and saturation values varies from application to application.

There are several different names for color spaces that use intensity, hue, and saturation values. You might see **HSV**, which stands for "hue, saturation, value," or **HLS**, which stands for "hue, lightness, saturation."

2

Hardware Basics

In this chapter, I'll talk about how to get all those neat pictures you'll soon be creating out of the computer so that you can see them. It's useful to understand some hardware basics because they affect what we might want to do, and how we go about it. There will also be some buzzwords that are worth learning. We'll talk in some detail about CRTs and display controllers, because understanding these sheds light on restrictions and artifacts that might otherwise seem arbitrary. We'll also briefly mention the kinds of output technologies that can be found in well-equipped offices.

DISPLAY (CRT) BASICS

This section is about the **cathode ray tube** (CRT), probably the most common means for making computer graphics visible. You may be used to calling this device a **monitor**. A monitor is really the whole unit that includes the outer shell, internal electronics, on/off switch, front-panel twiddle knobs, and so on. The CRT is the "screen" part, where you see the picture.

What Is a Cathode-Ray Tube?

The CRT is one of the few types of vacuum tubes still in common use today. It works on the principle that some materials, called **phosphors**, emit light if you crash enough electrons into them. The face of a black-and-white CRT (we'll get to color shortly) is made of transparent glass coated on the inside with a continuous layer of this phosphor material. The rest of the CRT's job is to allow control over how many electrons hit the phosphor, and where they hit it.

A spot on the phosphor lights up more brightly as more electrons hit it. It starts getting dimmer when electrons stop hitting it. It stops emitting light only a short time later.

The **electron gun** produces a thin stream of electrons. The electron flow rate, also called the **beam current**, is controlled by the monitor's electronics. The stronger the beam current, the more brightly the phosphor spot will light. The **deflection yoke** magnetically steers the electron stream so that it hits the phosphor at the desired spot. The deflection yoke is also under control of the monitor's electronics. (See Figure 2.1.)

FIGURE 2.1 Cathode-ray-tube diagram.
A thin stream of electrons is produced by the electron gun, which is aimed at a particular spot on the screen by the deflection yoke. The inside of the screen is coated with phosphors that light up when hit by the electron beam.

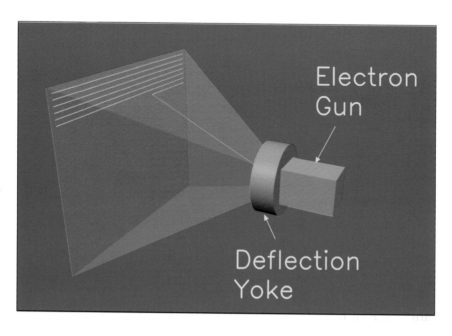

So, all a CRT really does is cause a selectable spot on its screen to shine with a selectable brightness.

Raster Scan

When you look at a CRT monitor, you don't just see a few lit dots—you see whole areas lit. How is that done?

The dot that can be lit up is rapidly swept across the CRT face (by re-aiming the electron beam) in a pattern called a **raster scan**. The dot typically starts at the top left corner. It's then swept across to the top right corner. The electron beam is temporarily shut off while it's redirected to the left side of the screen. The beam then scans across the screen just a little below the previous scan line. This process continues until the beam finally sweeps the bottom scan line; then the whole process is repeated.

An image is formed on the monitor screen by modulating the beam current as the lit dot is moved around. High beam currents make bright areas, and low beam currents make dim areas. The raster scan pattern maps nicely to the pixels in an image. Each horizontal traverse of the beam displays one horizontal row of pixels. The pixel values within each scan line are used to control the beam current as the beam sweeps across the screen.

Figure 2.1 shows six whole scan lines, with the seventh still being drawn. The point of a raster scan is to eventually hit every spot on the screen, so the scan lines overlap a little. Figure 2.1 shows spaces between the scan lines only to help you understand a raster scan.

Why don't we just see a dot flying around the screen instead of whole areas lit? There are two reasons for this. First, your eyes continue to perceive light for a short time after the light has gone away. This is called **persistence of**

vision. Second, a phosphor spot keeps glowing a little while after the beam goes away. This is called **phosphor persistence.** Therefore, as long as the spot is swept over the whole screen fast enough, it will appear as a steady area of light instead of a flying spot of light.

How fast is fast? Today's monitors typically scan the entire screen 60 to 80 times per second. If they went much slower, the image would appear to flicker.

Color

I can hear you thinking, *I can almost believe this, but how is color possible? After all, electron beams don't come in different colors.* No, they don't. What I've described so far is how black-and-white CRTs work. The basic process doesn't really support color. To get color, engineers have come up with some strange kludges and hacks. It's amazing to me that color CRTs work at all.

Although electron beams don't come in different colors, phosphors do. To make a color CRT, little phosphor dots for each of the three primary colors (red, green, blue) are arranged on the monitor screen. Then, three electron guns are used, one for each phosphor color.

The tricky part is to make sure each electron gun can hit only the phosphor dots for its color. This is done by arranging three dots of different colors in groups, called **triads.** Because there are now three electron beams coming from three separate guns, each hits the phosphors from a slightly different angle. A thin sheet called the **shadow mask** is suspended in front of the phosphors. The shadow mask has one hole for each triad, and it is arranged so that each beam can "see" only the phosphor dots for its color. Take a look at Figure 2.2. In case that just sounds too flaky to be true, see Figure 2.3.

It's important not to confuse phosphor triads with pixels. Pixels are the individual color values that make up the image

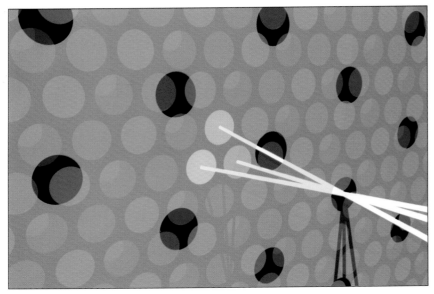

FIGURE 2.2 CRT shadow mask and phosphor dots.
The shadow mask is a thin sheet, shown here as semitransparent, suspended in front of the phosphor dots. There is one hole in the shadow mask for each phosphor triad, even though it may not appear that way in this picture due to the perspective. Because the three electron beams go through the shadow mask holes from slightly different angles, each beam can light up only the dots for its color. The three white lines represent the electron beams passing through a shadow mask hole to light up the center triad.

 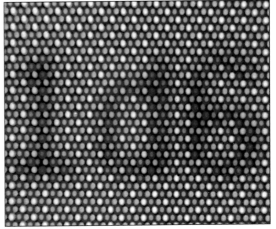

FIGURE 2.3 CRT photographs.
These pictures are actual photographs of a color CRT face. The left picture shows the whole screen, whereas the right picture was taken from a small region near the center that was displaying the characters "1d6." Note how the image is really lots and lots of red, green, and blue dots. You see a continuous shade instead of dots because individual dots are too small to see at the normal viewing distance. Your eyes blend the dots together, much as in the left picture. Try looking closely at a color CRT with a magnifying lens or a jeweler's loupe.

stored in the computer. Phosphor triads are a hack to get CRTs to display colors. The whole mechanism of three beams, a shadow mask, and phosphor triads exists only to provide separate red, green, and blue color control over the lit spot on the CRT face. As long as there are enough triads so you can't see individual ones, you can think of the CRT face as being continuous. The triads are arranged in a hexagonal pattern, while pixels are in a rectangular pattern. A CRT could be made where the shadow mask and triads are rotated a bit from horizontal with little overall effect.

Does the whole mechanism of three beams, a shadow mask, and phosphor triads sound bizarre? It is. How do you make sure the three beams hit exactly the same spot as they are swept across the screen? What if they don't? What if the shadow mask is off a little and the beams don't hit the spots for their colors? Well, these are real problems.

The degree to which all three beams line up to converge to one spot is called **convergence**. A monitor that is poorly converged looks blurry and shows color fringes around the edges of objects.

The degree to which each beam hits only the phosphor dots for its color is called **color purity**. If a CRT has poor color purity, colors will look less vivid, and there may be patches of tint here and there. For example, the top right corner may be more reddish, whereas the top left corner is more greenish.

This whole setup is very sensitive to magnetic fields because they can affect the electron beam paths. To prevent metal in the monitor chassis from becoming magnetic, any built-up magnetism must be periodically removed. This process is called **degaussing** and is usually done automatically every time the monitor is turned on. Listen for a low hum lasting about a second right after a monitor is switched on.

Why Do We Care?

A basic understanding of what's going on inside a CRT can be a big help when you buy color CRT monitors. In this section I'll briefly go over the CRT buzzwords you may see in catalogs or hear from sales representatives.

Keep in mind that while many sales reps are quite knowledgeable, there are also far too many who don't understand what they're talking about. Unfortunately, it's up to you to speak the "second language" of hardware specs, and to sort fact from fiction.

In general, any specification is measured to appear as favorable as possible, as long as there is a remote justification for doing so. It would be nice if specifications were written for what end users really get. Yeah, right.

Size   Monitor sizes are measured in screen diagonal length. Computer monitor sizes typically range from about 12 to 21 inches. You might think that on a 12-inch monitor the upper-right image corner would be 12 inches from the lower-left image corner. Unfortunately, it's not that simple.

I'm writing this on a 17-inch monitor, but I measure only $16^{1}/_{4}$ inches between opposite inside corners of the bezel surrounding the screen. That's because 17 inches is the size of the bare CRT, not the final displayable area that I get to see. The monitor manufacturer buys 17-inch CRTs and therefore claims to sell 17-inch monitors.

Worse yet, I can't even use all $16^{1}/_{4}$ inches of the visible CRT face. Many computer displays have a 5:4 aspect ratio, meaning they are four-fifths as tall as they are wide. Example 5:4 resolutions are 640×512, $1,024 \times 820$, $1,280 \times 1,024$, and $1,600 \times 1,280$. After adjusting the image to the largest possible 5:4 area, I am left with only a $15^{1}/_{4}$-inch diagonal. I guess this means $15^{1}/_{4} = 17$ in marketing math.

Dot Pitch   **Dot pitch** indicates how closely spaced the individual phosphor triads are, which relates to the smallest detail the CRT can possibly show, or resolve. (In practice, monitor resolution is dependent on many parameters.) Remember that there is one shadow mask hole for every color triad (review Figure 2.2). The CRT can't resolve anything smaller than the distance between adjacent shadow mask holes. This distance is what's called the *dot pitch*, even though it refers to triads, not dots.

The triads are arranged in a hexagonal pattern so that each triad has six neighbors. The distance to each of these neighbors is the dot pitch. See Figure 2.4 for a diagram of all this.

Typical dot pitch values are in the .2- to .3-millimeter range.

Triads versus Pixels   There seems to be much confusion among computer users about the distinction between triads

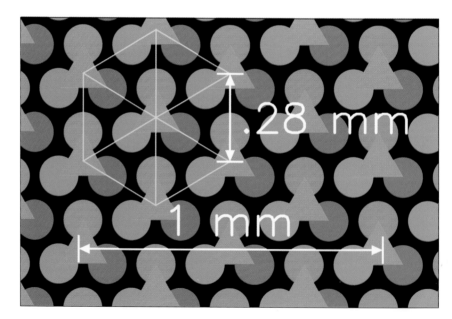

FIGURE 2.4 Monitor dot pitch measurement. This diagram shows how a monitor's dot pitch is measured. The monitor in this example has a dot pitch of .28 millimeters. The gray triangles mark triads so that you can see them more easily. The "cartwheel" in the upper left shows how each triad is the same distance from all six of its neighbors.

and pixels, and how they relate to each other. Remember that an image is a *rectangular* array of pixels (page 1). A quick look at Figure 2.4 should show you that pixels can't have a one-to-one relationship with triads because triads are arranged in a *hexagonal* pattern.

Phosphor triads are just a means of making a CRT display colors. But you can pretty much forget triads exist. They are deliberately too small to see so that they present the illusion of a continuous color screen.

Pixels, on the other hand, are the digital values used to drive the monitor's analog controls. Each horizontal row of pixels in the display hardware (we'll get into that on page 22) is used to modulate the electron beam currents for one horizontal sweep across the screen. The exact vertical placement of the beam sweeps, and the horizontal placement of individual pixels within each sweep, occurs without any regard to the placement, spacing, and orientation of the phosphor triads. In other words, pixels just fall where they fall, and it works because the screen can be thought of as continuous even though it happens to be made of lots of little dots. After all, most monitors have some diddle knobs that allow you to move the image up, down, left, and right, change its size, and sometimes even rotate it slightly. Clearly, pixels can be moved around without regard to the phosphor triads.

The spacing between phosphor triads, the dot pitch, does affect the monitor's maximum possible resolution. In other words, the visual detail in a color CRT image stops increasing as more pixels are used, once the pixel spacing is about the same as the triad spacing. For example, let's consider a monitor with a dot pitch of .28 millimeters. This means the closest spacing between triads is .28 millimeters, which means there are no more than 36 triads per centimeter, or 91 triads per inch. If you've got a 1,280 × 1,024 display, that means your monitor needs to be at least

14 inches wide to truly resolve all the pixels. This comes out to a diagonal display area size of 18 inches, which would require at least a "19-inch" monitor to achieve. (More marketing math!) In practice, the advantage of denser pixels doesn't suddenly stop when the dot pitch is reached, but it does start to seriously fall off. You will probably still perceive a better image at 1,280 × 1,024 pixels on a 17-inch monitor with .28 dot pitch than at 1,024 × 800 pixels. But, it's unlikely this would be true on a 12-inch monitor with a .28 dot pitch.

Scan (or Refresh) Rate   **Scan rate**, or **refresh rate**, refers to how fast the electron beams are swept across the screen. There are really two scan rates: horizontal and vertical. The *horizontal scan rate* is the rate at which individual scan lines are drawn; this rate is of little interest to end users. Users are more concerned with how many scan lines there are and how often the whole screen is refreshed. Typical horizontal scan rate values are in the 15- to 100-kilohertz range (15,000 to 100,000 times per second).

The *vertical scan rate* indicates how often the entire image is refreshed. This directly affects how much the image will appear to flicker. Most people will perceive a monitor image to be flicker-free at vertical scan rates of 60 to 70 hertz (60 to 70 times per second) and higher.

You may be able to see a monitor flicker by looking at it out of the corner of your eyes. Humans are more sensitive to flicker at the periphery of vision than at the spot at which they are directly looking. Try this with a regular (nondigital) television, which flickers at 60 hertz in North America and Japan, and 50 hertz most everywhere else. A flicker rate of 50 hertz is so low that many people can see the flicker even when looking directly at the screen.

Interlacing   A monitor running in interlaced mode refreshes only every other scan line each vertical pass. This means the entire image is refreshed every two vertical passes.

Why go to all that trouble? The apparent flicker you see comes from the vertical refresh rate, whether all the scan lines or only half are displayed each pass. For the same apparent flicker, interlacing requires only half as many scan lines to be drawn. This reduces the data rate and relaxes requirements on the monitor and graphics hardware electronics, saving money. Each vertical pass during which half the scan lines are drawn is called a **field**. The field containing the top scan line is called the **even field,** and the other is called the **odd field.** Both fields together, meaning all the scan lines drawn once, are called a **frame**. (See Figure 2.5.)

Briefly, interlacing is a means of reducing monitor and display hardware cost, while displaying the same image with

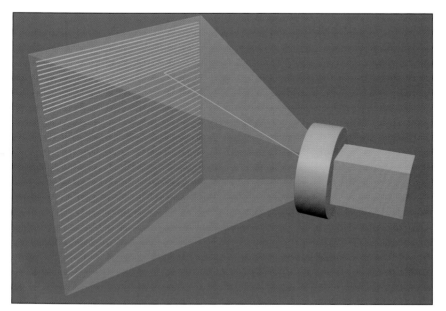

FIGURE 2.5 Scan line interlacing.
This diagram shows a frame being drawn partway through the second, or odd, field. The first, or even, field scan lines are shown in gray, while the odd field scan lines are shown in yellow. Note how each scan line is drawn halfway between two scan lines of the previous field.

the same apparent flicker. However, there's no free lunch. Thin horizontal lines in the image will flicker quite noticeably. Because they are on only one scan line, they get refreshed at only half the vertical refresh rate. Also, interlacing introduces one more thing that can go wrong. The image will be of poor quality if the beam sweeps of each vertical pass aren't exactly halfway between each other.

OTHER INTERACTIVE OUTPUT TECHNOLOGIES

Flat Panel

A flat panel display is any display that is much less thin than it is wide or tall. The main attraction is that flat panel displays take up less space than CRTs, although flat panels are also lighter and more rugged, consume less power, and have crisper displays. This makes them attractive for a variety of applications where these features are important, such as in portable computers.

A number of competing technologies can achieve flat displays, but all still cost significantly more than CRTs. However, flat panels should not be thought of as mere replacements to CRTs. Their own unique blend of features has opened application areas inaccessible to CRTs, as in battery-operated or portable equipment, for example. As these application areas grow, volumes will increase and prices will drop. Also, new flat panel technologies continue to emerge. Eventually, some form of flat panel will replace the CRT in desktop applications where space, power, weight, and ruggedness aren't that important. Industry experts disagree on when this will happen. Conservative estimates are that half the units sold in these applications won't be flat panels until 2005 or maybe as late as 2010.

Head-Mounted Displays

A head-mounted display is any display that is fixed to your head and therefore moves with it. Usually, small, lightweight CRTs are built into a helmet, with the necessary optics so that it appears you are looking at a large screen.

If a separate display is provided for each eye, then you can see things in true 3D. Now imagine that the computer can sense your head position and orientation, then update the displays in real time. The computer can now create the illusion of three-dimensional objects that exist in fixed space as you move. With the addition of position-sensitive input devices on your hands, you can interact with the computer in a 3D virtual, visual world. This has been given the rather pretentious name of **virtual reality**. (What will they call it when we have smell and full-body-touch feedback?) Applications range from entertainment to data visualization to remote robotics.

HARD COPY

Hard-copy output is loosely defined as something you can walk away with and don't need a computer to view. Examples are a paper printout or a photograph. In this section I'll very briefly talk about some of the common hard-copy technologies and devices.

Printers

Printers are used to create hard-copy output on paper or overhead transparencies. Products are available in a wide quality/price range. I'll mention the common ones relevant to computer graphics.

Inkjet   Inkjet printers squirt tiny drops of ink onto the page. A measure of quality is how close together the ink dots can be, usually specified in dots per inch (**DPI**). Common values range from 300 to over 700 DPI. These types of printers are relatively inexpensive, but slow. Image quality can be moderate to good, especially at the higher dot resolutions.

Laser Printers   Laser printers work much like photocopiers. A rotating drum picks up little particles, called **toner**, where light didn't hit the drum (how the drum does this is beyond the scope of this book). A piece of paper is then squished against the drum, which transfers the toner to the paper. The paper and toner are then heated and squished again to keep the toner from coming off on your hand later.

In photocopiers, the drum is illuminated by an image of the original document. Toner ends up on the copy wherever no light hit the drum, meaning the original had a black mark. In laser printers, a laser scans the drum as it rotates. The output paper will be left blank where the laser was switched on, and toner will be deposited where the laser was switched off.

Laser printers are more expensive than inkjet printers, but they are usually much faster.

Wax Transfer   Wax transfer printers press a thin sheet of wax-coated plastic against a special paper, then selectively heat the plastic as it passes over a row of heating elements. The wax transfers to the paper where the plastic is heated and stays on the plastic where no heat was applied.

More detail isn't relevant because advances in inkjet and laser printers are grabbing market share from wax transfer printers. Wax transfer printers are usually a bit more expensive than laser printers. Image quality can be reasonably good, and speed is comparable to that of midrange to low-end laser printers. However, the per-page cost is often ten times that of laser printers and inkjet printers.

Dye Sublimation   Dye sublimation printers produce the ultimate in image quality, at a premium in price. They work somewhat like wax transfer printers. Instead of transferring wax from a ribbon to the paper, dye is evaporated from the ribbon, then condensed, or sublimated, onto the paper. The amount of evaporated dye can be accurately controlled, giving a variable intensity instead of an on or off for each dot. The resulting output is comparable in quality to the prints you get when you have your film developed and processed at the photo store.

This technology is still maturing and coming down in price, but it will likely remain much more expensive than inkjet for some time. Currently, dye sublimation printers cost about 10 to 20 times what inkjets cost. Per-page costs are around 15 to 30 times those of inkjets.

Film Recorders

Film recorders are devices for writing computer images onto film. Typical output formats are 35mm slides or negatives, or instant prints.

The most common type is a camera pointed at a black-and-white CRT with a set of selectable color filters in between. The red image component is displayed with a red filter in front of it, then the green component with a green filter, then the same for blue. The final image on the film is the sum of everything it sees over the whole time the shutter is open.

DISPLAY CONTROLLER BASICS

A **display controller** is a piece of computer hardware that takes drawing commands from the processor and drives the display. This is often called the **video card** or **graphics card**. See Figure 2.6. A display controller outputs the video signals for the monitor.

The bitmap is the heart of any display controller: It is where the pixels are kept. The bitmap divides the remaining display controller into the drawing "front end" and the video "back end." We'll talk about those first, then get back to some more bitmap details.

Drawing "Front End"

The **front end**, or drawing engine, receives drawing commands from the processor. The front end figures out

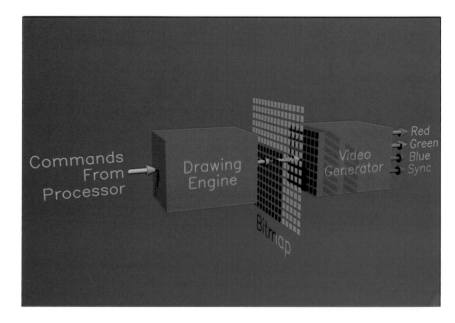

FIGURE 2.6 Display controller block diagram.
The main display controller components are the drawing engine, bitmap, and video generator. These are described in the following sections.

which pixels are being drawn and what color, or value, they should be. The pixels are "drawn" by writing the new values into the bitmap.

The drawing command set can vary greatly from one display controller to another. To give you some idea, a typical command sequence for drawing a red rectangle from 15,10 to 34,24 might be as follows:

1. Set current fill color to red.

2. Set current point to 15,10.

3. Draw rectangle, width = 20, height = 15.

Most display controllers also allow the processor to directly read and write the pixels in the bitmap. The processor could have directly written red into all the pixels from 15,10 to 34,24 to write the same rectangle as before. However, the purpose of the drawing engine is to off-load this kind of work from the processor. Not only can the drawing engine do this task faster, the processor can go do something else once the drawing engine gets started on the rectangle.

Video "Back End"

The job of the video **back end** is to interpret the bitmap pixel values into their colors and to create the video signals that drive the monitor so you can see the colors. The bitmap values are reread each time the monitor image is refreshed. Because this typically happens 60 to 80 times per second, the bitmap is effectively displayed "live."

Color Lookup Tables (LUTs)   I mentioned before that one of the video back end's jobs is to interpret the bitmap pixel values into their resulting colors. This sounds a little silly.

Why aren't the colors just stored in the bitmap directly? The main reason is to require less bitmap memory. A secondary reason is to allow some correction for the weird things monitors can do to colors and brightness levels.

So how does going through an interpretation step save memory? Let's look at what it would take to store color values directly. As I mentioned before (see page 2, "Colors and Color Spaces"), it takes three numbers to describe a color. The standards for video signals that drive computer monitors use the RGB color space, so the three numbers would need to be the red, green, and blue color components. In computer graphics, we think of RGB color components as being "continuous" (you can't distinguish individual levels anymore) when there are at least 256 levels per RGB component. Because 256 levels requires 8 bits ($2^8 = 256$), or 1 byte, a full color requires 3 bytes. If your bitmap has a resolution of 1,024 × 800 pixels, that would require about 2.5 megabytes for the bitmap. Memory usually comes in standard sizes, so you'd probably end up with 4 megabytes in your bitmap. (No, this isn't stupidity. There are good reasons for this, but they're beyond the scope of this book.)

The cost of low-end graphics boards is usually dominated by the cost of the bitmap memory, so we'd like to reduce the amount of this memory. Three bytes per pixel lets us store any color in any pixel, but do we really need this? Unless you are doing imaging, the answer is usually no. Look at a typical screen with a few windows, text, and menus. How many *different* colors do you see? Probably not more than 16. Suppose we numbered each of these colors from 0 to 15. We would then need only 4 bits per pixel in the bitmap, but we'd have to interpret the color numbers into their real colors to generate the final RGB video signals.

In practice, we usually use 8 bits per pixel instead of the 4 in the example. Eight bits allow up to 256 different colors on the screen at the same time. That's more than enough for the basic user interface, plus it allows some way to see images, support games, and so on. Two hundred fifty-six simultaneous colors requires 1 byte per pixel. The entire $1,024 \times 800$ bitmap would then fit into just 1 megabyte with room to spare. Note that we've reduced the bitmap memory from 4 megabytes to 1 megabyte at a price. First, we can display only 256 colors simultaneously, and second, we now have to interpret the color numbers into real RGB colors.

The interpretation job is done in the **color lookup table**, often called the **LUT**. The LUT converts the color numbers, usually called the **color index values** or **pseudo colors**, from the bitmap into their assigned RGB colors. In our example, the LUT has 256 entries because that's how many possible color index values there are. Each entry holds a 24-bit (8 bits per color component) RGB value.

True Color, Pseudo Color   A system that stores RGB values directly in the bitmap is called a **true color system**, and one that stores color index values is called a **pseudo color system**. Figures 2.7 and 2.8 show how the final displayed color value is determined for each pixel.

While a lookup table is required in a pseudo color system, many true color systems also use them. In that case, they can be used to compensate for some artifacts introduced by the monitor or for special effects. In practice, most true color lookup tables are just loaded with "straight through" data, and you can usually forget them.

Let's look at the examples in Figures 2.9 and 2.10 to make sure the true color versus pseudo color distinction makes sense.

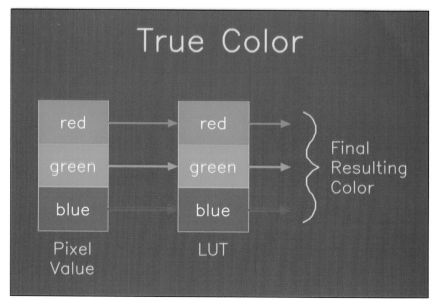

FIGURE 2.7 True color interpretation.
True color is the conceptually simple color configuration. The actual, or "true," pixel color is stored directly in each pixel. The color lookup table, or LUT, is not necessary in a true color system. It is usually present because most true color systems also support pseudo color where the LUT is needed. In true color mode, the LUT is usually loaded with values so that it has no net effect. It is sometimes used to compensate for artifacts introduced by monitors and for special effects.

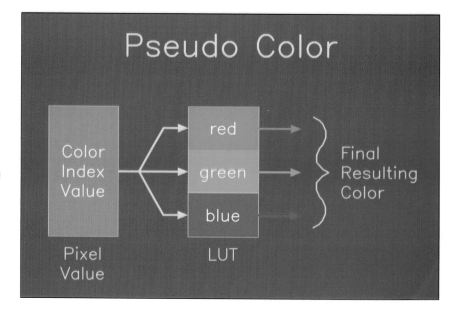

FIGURE 2.8 Pseudo color interpretation.
In a pseudo color configuration, each pixel holds an index into the color lookup table instead of a true color value. The color lookup table is required to convert the color index values into the true RGB color values.

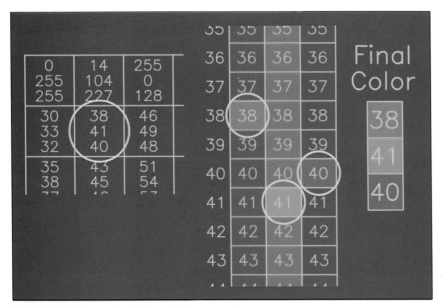

FIGURE 2.9 True color interpretation example.
In this example we are trying to determine what the final visible color is for the circled bitmap pixel on the left. Because this is a true color example, each pixel contains separate red, green, and blue values. In this case there are 8 bits per color component per pixel, so color components range from 0 to 255. The selected pixel contains red 38, green 41, and blue 40. The corresponding LUT entries are found (the left column on the blue background) separately for each of the color components. The resulting final color values from the LUT are circled and shown on the right.

Note that in this example the LUT values are such that the final color is the same as the pixel values. This is usually the case in true color because there's usually no need for an additional interpretation step between the pixel values and the final color values.

Bitmap

The **bitmap** is the two-dimensional array of pixels that the drawing front end writes into and that the video back end reads from. Because frequent and high-speed access to the bitmap is required, it is always (except for some rare specialty systems) implemented as a separate memory right in the display controller. You have no reason to care how the bitmap is implemented; only the price and performance of the overall display controller need concern you.

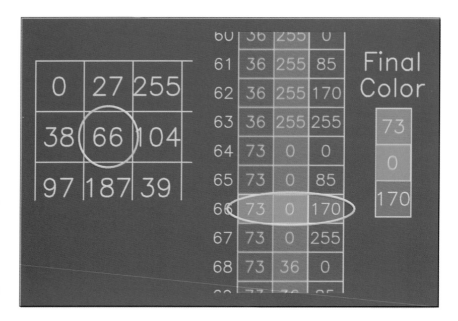

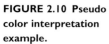

FIGURE 2.10 Pseudo color interpretation example.
In this example, a pseudo color is converted to a final color value. The pseudo color value from the selected pixel is 66. Therefore, the final color value is taken from LUT entry 66 for all color components, as shown.

DRAM versus VRAM   Although you shouldn't have to care, you can sometimes choose between **DRAM** and **VRAM**. What are they, and what do they do for you?

DRAM stands for Dynamic Random Access Memory. I won't go into what that means, except that DRAM is the "normal" kind of memory that is also used to make the main memory in your computer. VRAM stands for Video Random Access Memory and is specifically designed to function as bitmap memory.

The drawing front end can independently write into a VRAM bitmap while the video back end is reading the pixels. In a DRAM bitmap, the front and back ends have to share. In some DRAM configurations, the back end can hog the bitmap up to 80 percent of the time. This doesn't leave much for the front end and slows down drawing operations. Of course, there's always a trade-off, which in this case is price.

VRAMs cost about twice what DRAMs cost for the same amount of memory.

What do I recommend getting? That's like asking whether I recommend a station wagon or a sports car. In general, though, I wouldn't shell out the extra moola for VRAM unless I knew I'd be running drawing-limited applications where performance is important. If you're not sure about that, just get DRAM.

What's in Hardware and What's in Software

Take another look at Figure 2.6. Note that the drawing engine isn't absolutely necessary as long as the processor has direct access to the bitmap. Such a system wouldn't need to lack features. It would be low-cost but slow. At the other extreme, a system might have full hardware support for everything from simple lines to fancy 3D operations and drawing commands. This would be faster but more expensive.

In practice, even low-end systems usually have hardware support for simple 2D drawing. The incremental cost of adding such a drawing engine is small compared to the bitmap and the video back-end cost. Such a system is sometimes referred to as a **2D display controller** or graphics board, or **GUI engine**. GUI (pronounced goo-ee) stands for *graphical user interface* and refers to these kinds of operations.

There are systems available with just about any imaginable trade-off between what's in hardware and what the software must do. Marketing types, however, like fancy labels to make their product sound more sophisticated than the next one. Some "standard" names have emerged for some configurations. I'll make you aware of them, but keep in mind this is a moving target because companies can (and often do) make up new names and use old names in new ways.

I've already mentioned the 2D or GUI engine. This usually means a minimal drawing engine that's good at simple 2D lines, points, rectangles, pixel copies, and maybe some polygons (we'll get into what these are in the next chapter). That's all that's needed by most window systems for menus, text, pop-ups, and more.

A 2½D display controller is intended for drawing 3D objects, but it doesn't have true 3D capability. It provides the 2D support needed for 3D drawing. This usually includes allowing the color to vary across the object being drawn (called *bilinear interpolation*, explained on page 127), *dithering* (page 148), and *Z buffering* (page 96).

A full **3D display controller** understands true 3D commands. It must do transformations, lighting, and other advanced effects that don't make sense to talk about until you've read Chapter 7, "Rendering."

Technology keeps marching on. In the current trend, the cost of logic for implementing drawing engines is falling faster than the cost of the bitmap and the video back end. If this continues, we will see ever more capable low-end systems. Who knows what tomorrow brings?

3

Graphic Primitives

WHAT'S A GRAPHIC PRIMITIVE?

One example of a graphic primitive is a Neolithic hunter making handprints on a cave wall, but that's not the meaning I had in mind. In computer graphics, a **graphic primitive** is something we know how to draw directly into a bitmap, such as a line, a point, and some polygons.

More complicated objects are drawn by using multiple primitives. Figure 3.1 was drawn from 12 polygons. In this case the primitives are fairly large and obvious. You can probably count them yourself. Keep in mind that not all the polygons are visible.

For a more complicated object, see Figure 3.2. This image was made from about 72,000 triangles, although it's not possible to pick out any one of them. In computer graphics we usually get complex shapes by using lots and lots of simple building blocks.

There'll be more on how to build neat shapes in the modeling chapter. For now, we need to understand the basic primitives at our disposal.

POINT

What's there to say about a **point primitive**—it's just a dot, right? Yeah, mostly. Sometimes, however, we have to think

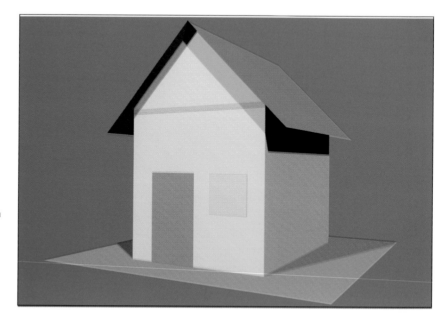

FIGURE 3.1 Simple compound object.
This object was drawn with 12 primitives, which were 10 quadrilaterals and 2 pentagons. In many graphics systems, these would be further decomposed into triangles.

FIGURE 3.2 More complicated compound object.
This image of a Chrysler Laser was made from about 72,000 triangles.
Data courtesy of Chrysler Corporation.

about how big the dot is. In math class we were told a point is infinitely thin. In computer graphics the smallest thing we can draw directly is a pixel. A point is often drawn as one pixel, but we might also use a small clump of pixels. Some interfaces allow the user or application to specify a "dot width."

VECTOR

A computer graphics **vector primitive** is just a line segment. It is called a vector mostly for historical reasons. (Beware that the term *vector* is also used in a more mathematical sense, as defined on page 40.) As with point primitives, vector primitives have a finite width. Vectors are often drawn by choosing just one pixel from each row or column (whichever way prevents skipping pixels). An interesting artifact of this is that diagonal vectors are represented by about 29 percent fewer pixels for the same length as vertical or horizontal vectors are. Many interfaces allow the user or application to set a fixed **vector thickness**. See Figure 3.3.

Polyline

A **polyline** is just a bunch of vectors drawn end to end, as shown in Figure 3.4. Each of the points in the polyline is specified only once. Because all but the first and last point are shared by two vectors, polylines can be handled more efficiently than an equivalent list of independent vectors.

Most vector-per-second specifications for display subsystems are for short vectors in long polylines. That's probably not what you'd be drawing, but remember, specs should be thought of only as the "guaranteed not to exceed" values.

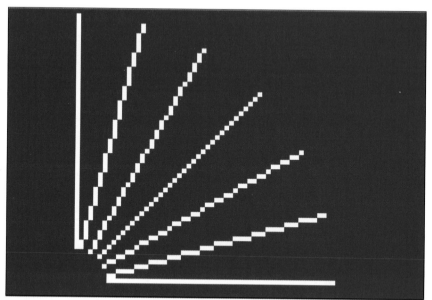

FIGURE 3.3 Simple 2D vector primitives.
Here's an example of seven simple vector primitives drawn into a very low resolution bitmap (90 × 60 pixels). Although each vector is the same length, note how the diagonal one has the fewest pixels (35), and the horizontal and vertical ones the most (49). This means that horizontal and vertical vectors of this type will appear brighter than diagonal ones when viewed from far enough away so that individual pixels can't be seen.

POLYGON

A mathematical polygon is a bunch of line segments connected end to end in a closed loop. In computer graphics, we usually care more about the surface inside the line segments, and generally mean that when we use the term **polygon**. Figure 3.5 shows some 2D examples.

An important property of a polygon is whether it is **convex** or **concave**. If you draw a line over a convex polygon, the line will cross the polygon only once, no matter where you draw the line. For a concave polygon, you can always find a line that crosses the polygon at least twice. Visually, this

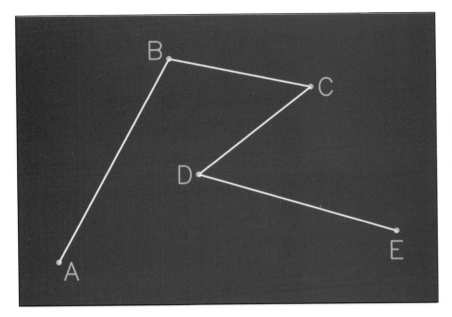

FIGURE 3.4 Polyline primitive.
This polyline contains four vectors, described by five points. The same net effect could be achieved by drawing the four vectors separately, but that would be less efficient because the computations for points B, C, and D would not be shared.

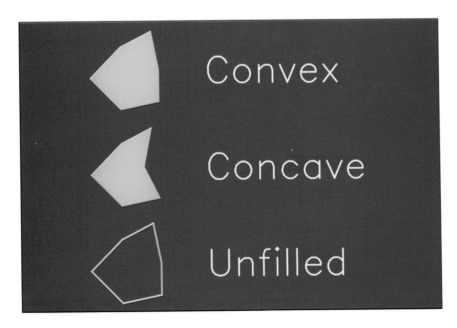

FIGURE 3.5 Examples of 2D polygon primitives.

means that convex polygons "bulge out" at all corners. Concave polygons have at least one corner that forms a dimple rather than a bulge.

Gee, that's great, but why do we care? Deep down, most graphics systems know how to draw only very simple convex polygons, usually triangles. (Trust me on this. The reasons why are beyond the scope of this book.) All other polygons have to be broken into an equivalent set of triangles in the software. This process is fairly easy for convex polygons, but a real pain for concave ones. It's also relatively complex to figure out whether an arbitrary list of points represents a convex or concave polygon. As a result, graphics systems either don't support concave polygons at all or make you tell them when a polygon might be concave. The concave polygons then take significantly longer to draw.

The moral? Think in terms of simple convex polygons. Better yet, think *triangles,* which are always convex and are the simplest polygons (only three corners). For this reason, triangles are used heavily. Many graphics systems have separate primitives for triangles that are more efficient than the general polygon primitives.

Triangle Strip

Particularly in 3D applications, we rarely draw just one triangle. Figure 3.2 was drawn with about 72,000 triangles. As in Figure 3.2, lots of abutting triangles are often used to draw curved surfaces. They are usually arranged in a regular mesh where six triangles meet at every corner. If each triangle is drawn individually, the shared corners would go through many of the same computations six times. Mesh and strip primitives are ways of avoiding or reducing this

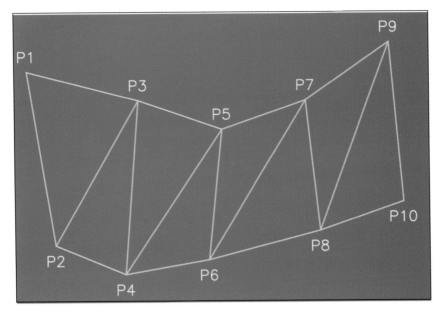

FIGURE 3.6 Triangle strip (Tstrip) primitive. After the first triangle, additional triangles are specified with only one point. For example, the point P4 causes the triangle P2-P3-P4 to be drawn. Point P5 causes the triangle P3-P4-P5 to be drawn. This process continues to the end of the triangle strip.

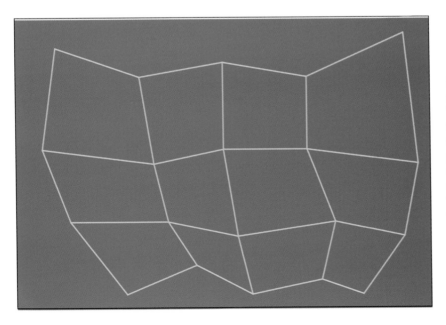

FIGURE 3.7 Quad mesh primitive. This primitive draws all the quadrilaterals defined by a grid of points. I'm showing the edges of the individual quadrilaterals here so that you can better see what's going on. Keep in mind, though, that this kind of primitive is often used to draw 3D surfaces. In that case the idea is to *not* see the individual quads.

overhead. They use much the same idea as the polyline primitive (page 33) extended to surfaces.

A **triangle strip** is one row, or "strip," of abutting triangles. These are often just called **Tstrips**. The triangles in a Tstrip abut in regular succession such that only one point is needed to specify each new triangle (see Figure 3.6). This allows the Tstrip to be stored, transmitted, and drawn efficiently.

Quad Mesh

A **quad mesh** is the same idea as a triangle strip, except that the primitives are quadrilaterals, and an entire mesh instead of just one strip is drawn. Quad meshes can be very efficient means to draw complicated surfaces that are defined by a rectangular grid of points. See Figure 3.7.

4

3D Vectors and Transforms

This chapter will give you an intuitive feel for what 3D (three-dimensional) vectors and 3D transforms are, and what kinds of things we can do with them. Don't worry, there won't be any heavy math because the actual equations really aren't that important anyway. What I want you to get out of this is a general, intuitive understanding.

　　If you're *really* allergic to math, you can skip this chapter and still profit from the rest of this book. However, you might want to at least flip through and look at the pictures. I've tried very hard to make this stuff understandable, even if you don't spend all your spare time calculating pi to the umpteenth decimal place.

3D VECTORS

This section introduces 3D vectors and shows some things we do with them in computer graphics. It is also a prerequisite for the next section on 3D transforms. If you already understand things such as normal vector, dot product, and cross product, then you can safely skip this section.

3D

3D stands for *three-dimensional,* as opposed to (at least in this book), **2D,** or *two-dimensional.* Two-dimensional objects are always flat because they have only two dimensions: width and height. Three-dimensional objects exist in a volume and have dimensions of width, height, and depth. For example, a rectangle drawn on a piece of paper is 2D, whereas a cardboard box is 3D.

Three-dimensional objects are defined in a 3D coordinate space. Just as you use X and Y to plot a point on a 2D graph, we use X, Y, and Z as the coordinates of a point in 3D. For example, you can use 2D coordinates to tell someone you see a rabbit 20 meters forward and 10 meters to the right. But for a bird you might use 3D by saying it's 20 meters forward, 10 meters to the right, and 15 meters up. We'll get into more detail about 3D coordinate spaces on page 49.

What's a Vector?

The word *vector* can have lots of different meanings. To some people it means a small buzzing insect that infects you with malaria, yellow fever, communism, or whatever. In computer graphics, however, a **vector** is just a fancy math term for a direction and a length. "Two miles east" is an example of a vector. It's also important to remember that a vector doesn't have a position. For example, "two miles east from my house" isn't a vector.

A vector is also sometimes said to describe a **displacement**. A displacement is just a distance traveled in a particular direction. I may drive 5 miles to work, but end up at a displacement of only 3 miles southeast from my house. If I drive in a loop, I end up with a displacement of zero.

Believe it or not, ordinary numbers also have a special name—to distinguish them from vectors, I suppose. In math terms, regular numbers are **scalars**. (I guess the term "number" isn't sufficiently lofty when used in research papers and grant proposals.)

Note that a 3D vector has three degrees of freedom and therefore requires three numbers of storage inside a computer. The direction takes up two degrees of freedom, and the length takes up the third. You can convince yourself that a direction has two degrees of freedom by thinking about aiming a cannon. The compass direction in which the cannon is pointing is one degree of freedom; how high the cannon is pointing is the second. (See Figure 4.1.)

Normal Vector   A **normal vector** is a vector that's pointing straight out from (at right angles to) something else, usually a surface we are trying to draw. As far as I know, there is no such thing as an abnormal vector. In this case, *normal* is a math term for "at right angles to." You can think of a normal vector as pointing in the direction a surface is facing. This will come in handy later when we try to figure out how much a surface is facing toward the light source. (See Figure 4.2.)

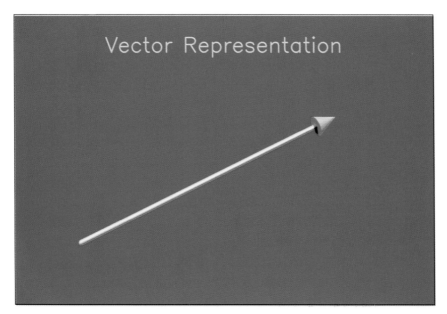

FIGURE 4.1 Vector depiction.
You might think this is a vector, but it's really just an arrow. Because a vector is only a direction and a length, it doesn't have a shaft or a pointy head. Because arrows also have a length and point in a particular direction, vectors are often depicted as arrows. That's what we'll do, too.

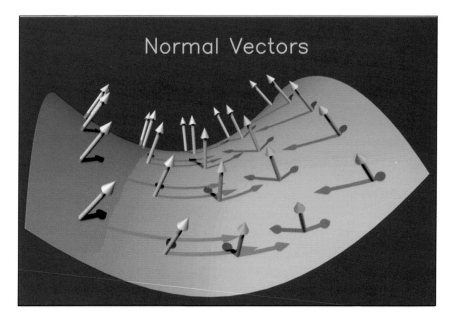

FIGURE 4.2 Normal vector example.
The arrows represent vectors that are at right angles to (normal to) the curved surface. They indicate which way the surface is facing.

Vector Operations

In this section, we'll talk about all the fun things we do with vectors in computer graphics (or at least those things we can talk about in public).

Vector Operation: Addition   The sum of two or more vectors is simply the sum of their displacements. Take a look at Figure 4.3.

Numerically, vectors are summed by individually summing all the X, Y, and Z components. In the example in Figure 4.3, X increases to the right, Y increases away, and Z increases up from the plane. The four vectors that are added together are $(-2, 1, 0)$, $(0, 0, 1)$, $(-1, -1, 0)$, and $(0, 0, -1)$. The sum of these vectors is $(-3, 0, 0)$. Take a moment and convince yourself these numbers correspond to what you see in Figure 4.3. Now separately add the X, Y, and Z components of the four vectors to see where $(-3, 0, 0)$ came from.

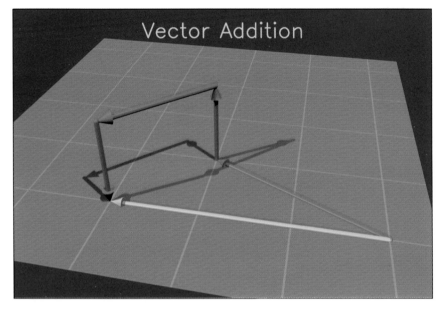

FIGURE 4.3 Vector addition example. In this example, the sum of the four green vectors is equal to the yellow vector. The vectors to be summed are arranged head to tail in a chain. The sum of all the vectors is the net displacement of the chain.

Vector Operation: Scaling   Vectors don't always come in the lengths you want them to. The **vector scaling** operation changes a vector's length by a scale factor without affecting its direction. For example, scaling the vector "2 miles east" by 3 yields "6 miles east." Yes, this really is as simple as it sounds.

Note that a vector's length may not be immediately obvious, depending on how it's defined. The lengths of vectors defined with angles and a distance are obvious. For example, "northwest, 1 furlong" clearly has a length of 1 furlong (whatever that is). In computer graphics, however, we usually manipulate vectors that are defined in components. The length of "east 1 furlong, north 1 furlong" may not be so obvious. It turns out the answer is about 1.4 furlongs.

One operation that comes up a lot in computer graphics is scaling a vector by the reciprocal of (1 divided by) its length, which always results in a unit vector (page 47). This operation is sometimes called **unitizing** the vector. For example, scaling "3 miles east" by ⅓ results in "1 mile east." (See Figure 4.4.)

Vector Operation: Similarity of Direction   It is often useful to know how much two vectors are pointing in the same direction. This happens, for example, when we try to figure out how much a surface is facing toward a light source. In more mathematical terms, we want to know how similar in direction the vector from the surface to the light source is with the surface normal vector. (See Figure 4.2 for a quick reminder of what normal vectors are.)

Fortunately, this similarity of direction is not too hard for the computer to find. We can get a number from 1 to −1, where 1 indicates the vectors are pointing in exactly the same direction, 0 means they are at right angles, and −1 means they are pointing in exactly opposite directions. In the example with the surface and the light source, a value of 1

FIGURE 4.4 Vector scaling example.
Vector scaling is simply changing the length of a vector by a scale factor. Note that scaling by a negative number flips the vector's direction. Scaling a vector by 1 divided by its length results in a unit vector. It is not possible to scale the original vector to end up with the one labeled with a question mark, because this vector is not parallel to the original vector.

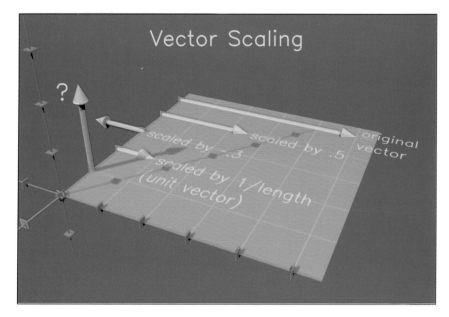

means the surface is facing directly toward the light. The surface is facing successively more away from the light (and therefore less light is illuminating the surface) as the value goes to 0. At 0, the light is exactly skimming the surface. This is much like sunset in Kansas. At values below 0, the surface is facing away from the light, and therefore none of the light is hitting the surface.

What I've been calling the "similarity of direction" operation is based on the **vector dot product**, which is a standard term used in math books that discuss vectors.

Before we talk about exactly what a general dot product is, let's define the dot product of two unit vectors (vectors that both have a length of 1). It turns out that this is simply the length of the projection of one vector onto the other. See Figure 4.5.

The dot product of two arbitrary vectors is the dot product of their unitized versions (−1 to 1 similarity of

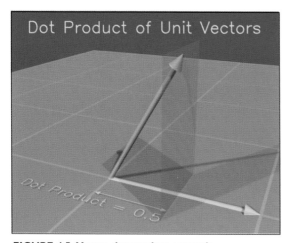 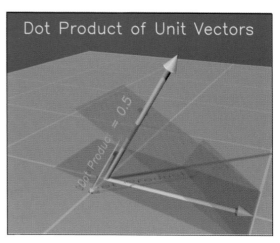

FIGURE 4.5 Vector dot product example.
The dot product of two unit vectors (vectors of length 1) is the length of the projection of one vector onto the other. As shown by the two images, it doesn't matter which vector is projected onto which. The dot product of two unit vectors is 1 when they point in the same direction, 0 when they are at right angles, and −1 when they point in opposite directions. The vectors in these images have a 60° degree angle between them, which results in a dot product of ½.

direction) times the original lengths of each of the two vectors. Therefore, if the bottom vector in Figure 4.5 were doubled in length, the dot product of the two vectors would be 1 instead of 0.5. If the top vector were also doubled, the dot product would double again to 2.0.

In computer graphics we are usually interested in the similarity of the direction of two vectors more than their pure dot product. This means we usually have to unitize the vectors or arrange for them to be of unit length in the first place. Unfortunately, unitizing a vector can be a bit of a pain for the computer. Calculating a dot product requires only three multiplies and two adds, whereas unitizing a vector requires six multiplies, two adds, one divide, and one square root. For this reason, we sometimes take pains to remember whether a vector has already been unitized because we don't want to perform such an expensive operation more often than necessary.

Vector Operation: Cross Product   Sometimes you need to find a vector that is at right angles (perpendicular) to two other vectors. This might happen if you need a surface normal vector, but have only two vectors pointing in different directions along the surface. The **vector cross product** operation can help.

The cross product of two vectors is always another vector (as opposed to the dot product, which produces just a number, or scalar), and this vector is always at right angles to both the original vectors. However, the length of the new vector depends on the length of the two original vectors and the angle between them. Because in computer graphics we usually do a cross product just to get the direction, I won't bother you with all the details of the resulting vector's length.

Cross products are also order-dependent. It turns out that **A** cross **B** is the negative (vector of same length but exactly

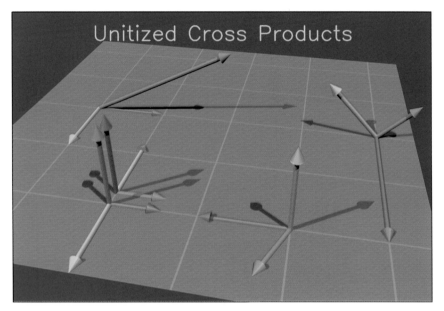

Unitized Cross Products

FIGURE 4.6 Vector cross product example. In each triplet of vectors, the yellow vector is the unitized result of the red vector cross the green vector. Note how the yellow vector is always at right angles to both the red and green vectors.

opposite direction) of **B** cross **A**. Because a picture is worth a thousand equations, see Figure 4.6.

Special Vectors

Some vectors have special properties or are used in particular circumstances so often that they have special names. Below are a few that we'll bump into a lot. We'll define some others in later chapters as we encounter them.

Unit Vector　A **unit vector** is simply a vector that has a length of 1. (Mathematicians and scientists often say "unit" when other people would just say "one.") Even though this may sound like a silly thing with a needlessly special name, unit vectors are actually quite useful.

Because a unit vector's length is always constant, you can think of a unit vector as a pure direction. Note that unit vectors have only two degrees of freedom because there is no choice (or freedom) about the length.

3D TRANSFORMS

This section will give you an intuitive understanding of how objects are moved, rotated, squashed, and otherwise distorted in ways nature never intended. Believe it or not, any number of these unnatural acts can be described by just one pile of 12 numbers called a **3D transform**.

You should have already skimmed—at least—through the previous section on 3D vectors before reading on; I'll describe 3D transforms in terms of 3D vectors.

Why 3D Transforms?

What are 3D transforms good for? Actually, they can be very useful and save a lot of work if you know how to apply them.

Imagine you are trying to model a car. You've created a really nice model for the right front wheel, but you aren't looking forward to repeating all that work three more times for the other wheels. You also entered all the coordinates for the wheel with (0,0,0) on the axle, whereas the rest of the car is defined with (0,0,0) somewhere else. Oops! Worse yet, you'll need to make changes in the wheel soon. You certainly don't want to make the same changes four times. What do you do?

This is where 3D transforms come to the rescue. The wheel can be referenced four times, each time with a different 3D transform applied. The transforms can convert from the wheel's coordinate space to the car's, move the wheels to the correct places, and flip them in mirror images between the left and right sides of the car.

This is just one example of how transforms can be handy. Now that I've got you convinced these things are actually useful, let's explain what they are and how they work.

What's a Coordinate Space?

This question isn't as dumb as it may sound. Yeah, I know, a coordinate space is a reference frame where we can plot points and so forth, but how do we *define* such a coordinate space?

Remember a science class where you had to plot temperature as a function of pressure, beakers left unbroken as a function of class time, or whatever. You started with a blank sheet of graph paper, but you couldn't start plotting points until you drew the axes and labeled them. This means you implicitly defined where each axis would start (0 beakers is the third grid line from the bottom of the page), and what its scale factor was (every four little boxes up is one more beaker).

Labeling the axes was essentially defining the coordinate space. In general, we will define a coordinate space by specifying the one point where all axes are 0, called the **origin**. Then, for each axis, we specify the direction and distance it takes to move +1 along that axis. That's all it takes.

Look, Just Four Vectors!

Now let's examine our coordinate space definition a little more closely. The "one point where all axes are 0" is a coordinate. For a 3D space, this is just three numbers. Each "direction and distance it takes to move +1 . . ." is a vector. For a 3D space there are three vectors (one for each axis), and each vector requires three numbers. This means a total of 12 numbers (3 for the coordinate, plus 9 for the vectors) are required to define a 3D coordinate space.

A vector that defines the +1 increment for an axis is important enough that it has been given the special name **basis vector**. See Figure 4.7 for a visual example of a coordinate space defined by an origin and three basis vectors. Note that while a basis vector always has a length of 1 in its own space, it can have any length in some other coordinate space.

Note that our coordinate space definition is really *relative*, not absolute. In other words, it's a way of defining a new coordinate space in terms of some existing, or old, space. After all, the origin and the basis vectors have to be defined in a space. Exactly what the existing space is or how it's defined doesn't matter for our purposes.

Because the origin of the new space is just the coordinates of a point in the old space, it can be thought of as the vector from the old space's origin to that point. Or you can think of it as the vector from the old space's origin to the new space's origin. Because this is the displacement of the

FIGURE 4.7 3D coordinate space. This 3D coordinate space is completely defined by a point and three vectors. The point, shown as the yellow sphere, anchors the 0 value for all three axes. Each vector describes what it means to travel +1 unit in its corresponding axis. This picture, and others in this book, uses red for the X axis, green for the Y axis, and blue for the Z axis.

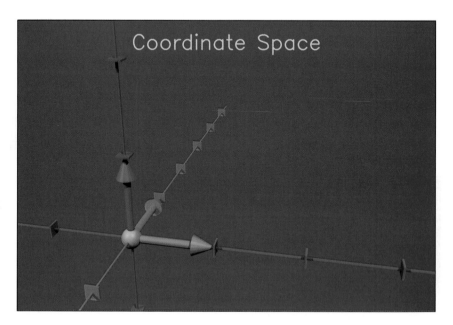

new space from the old, this is sometimes called the **displacement vector.**

To summarize, we can completely define a new 3D coordinate space relative to an old one using four vectors. These are the displacement vector and the three basis vectors, one for each axis. Figure 4.8 shows this visually.

For example, suppose you are having a house built in a town that uses a grid in miles to keep track of property. The southwest corner of your lot is at location 1.5, 0.7 on the town map, meaning it is 1.5 miles east and 0.7 miles north of the official reference point. However, to the builder, this coordinate system is cumbersome. He doesn't care much about where the plot is within the town, but rather where to build things within the lot. The builder defines his own coordinate system in feet, starting at the southwest corner of the lot. This is what he uses to place the house, the septic system, and the

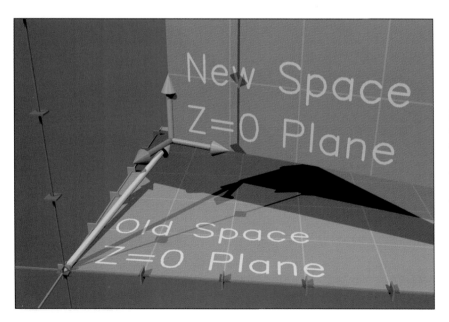

FIGURE 4.8 Relative coordinate space definition.
Four vectors are used to define a new 3D coordinate space in terms of an old one. The displacement vector is shown as a yellow arrow. The *X*-, *Y*-, and *Z*-axis basis vectors are shown as the red, green, and blue arrows, respectively.

pink flamingos. What the builder has done is create a new coordinate system relative to the town's. Keeping in mind that this is a 2D example and that there are 5,280 feet in a mile, the displacement vector is (1.5, 0.7), the X basis vector is ($1/5{,}280$, 0), and the Y basis vector is (0, $1/5{,}280$). Note that these values are *in terms of the old space.* By definition, the displacement vector is always (0,0), and the basis vectors are always (1,0) and (0,1) *from within their own space.*

Look, a 3D Transform!

So far, we've managed only to define one coordinate space in terms of another. What we really want to do is *convert* coordinates from one coordinate space to another. Fortunately, these are very closely related.

Let's review how we plot a point in the new space (or any space defined by an origin and basis vectors). It will make more sense if you follow the explanation visually in Figure 4.9.

First, we start at the origin of the new space (tip of the yellow arrow). Then we travel by the X basis vector scaled by our X coordinate (right-pointing gray arrow), the Y basis vector scaled by our Y coordinate (down-pointing gray arrow), and the Z basis vector scaled by our Z coordinate (gray arrow pointing toward us). We are now at the point we wanted to plot (white sphere). Keep in mind that because vector addition is not dependent on order, we didn't have to follow the X then Y then Z sequence.

We know that the coordinates of the point we plotted are (X, Y, Z) in the new space. The million-dollar question is, "What are the coordinates of this point in the old space?" As we'll see in the next section, these coordinates are found by following the same procedure we just used to plot the point. If the numerical values of the origin and basis vectors are

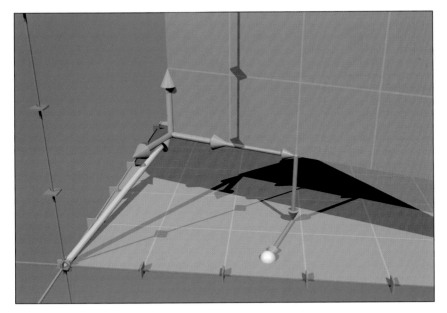

FIGURE 4.9 Plotting point (2, −1, 1).
The point (2, −1, 1) in the new space is plotted by starting at the new space's origin, then traveling two times its X basis vector (red), plus −1 times its Y basis vector (green), plus 1 times its Z basis vector (blue). The path taken is shown as gray arrows, with the final point shown as the white sphere.

expressed in the old space, then the resulting point will also be there. We'll do a complete example in the next section so you can see this in action.

The important thing to remember from this section is that we can use a relative coordinate space definition directly to transform points from the new space to the old. In fact, it turns out that the four vectors are exactly what's in a standard 3D transform. In math terms this is often called a **4 × 3 transformation matrix**; it is often written as just an array, or matrix, of 4 × 3 numbers.

Transforming a Point

In this section, we'll do a concrete numerical example of transforming a point from a new space to the old. The example uses the same values as Figure 4.9 so that you can follow along visually.

The four vectors defining the new coordinate space are: displacement vector (1, 2, 1), X basis vector (0.94, –0.34, 0), Y basis vector (0, 0, 1), and Z basis vector (–0.34, –0.94, 0). First, look at the picture and convince yourself that the yellow, red, green, and blue arrows do indeed reflect these values. Now we'll transform the point (2, –1, 1) from the new space to the old.

We start at the origin of the old space, which is (0, 0, 0). That's at the lower-left corner of the bottom grid. Then we add the displacement vector, which yields (1, 2, 1). This brings us to the tip of the yellow arrow. Now add X times the X basis vector, which is 2 times (0.94, –0.34, 0), or (1.88, –0.68, 0). (1, 2, 1) plus (1.88, –0.68, 0) brings us to (2.88, 1.32, 1). We are now at the tip of the first gray arrow. Y times the Y basis vector is –1 times (0, 0, 1), or (0, 0, –1). Adding this to our current location brings us to (2.88, 1.32, 0), which is at the tip of the second gray arrow. Finally, Z times the Z basis vector is 1 times (–0.34, –0.94, 0), which is simply (–0.34, –0.94, 0). This plus our current location yields (2.54, 0.38, 0), which is at the end of the third gray arrow and at the white ball.

We've done it. (2, –1, 1) in the new space is at the same location as (2.54, 0.38, 0) in the old space. Take a minute to look at Figure 4.9 and convince yourself this makes sense.

In math terms, we just transformed a point using a 4×3 transformation matrix.

Transforming a Vector

Transforming a vector is actually easier than transforming a point. Because a vector has no absolute location, only direction and length, we simply ignore the displacement vector. Otherwise the process is the same as transforming a point. Because we take only the three basis vectors into account, we are using only nine numbers instead of twelve. In math terms this is a 3 × 3 transformation matrix (instead of 4 × 3 when the displacement vector is used).

Merging Transforms

What if we defined a second coordinate space from an original space, then defined a third space from the second? What if we did this for a few more levels? Do we really need to keep track of this whole chain of transforms just to convert a point from the last space to the first?

Take a look at Figure 4.10. Here's an example of a second space defined in a first space, and a third defined in the second. To transform a point from the third space to the first, we already know how to transform it from the third to the second, then from the second to the first. But there is a better way.

After all, the vectors defining the third space also exist in the first space. This means we must be able to define the third

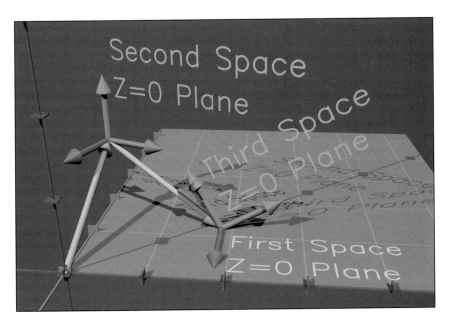

FIGURE 4.10 Nested coordinate spaces. The third coordinate space is defined in terms of the second coordinate space, which is defined in terms of the first coordinate space. Is there a way to go directly from the third space to the first space?

space directly from the first. Without going into all the gory details, remember that the third space is defined as a bunch of vectors in the second space. Because these are just vectors, we can transform them to the first space. (The displacement vector has to be handled a little differently, but that's too detailed to get into here.) Now we have a definition of the third space in terms of the first. That means we can transform a point directly from the third space to the first. This was done to Figure 4.10, yielding Figure 4.11.

We can do the same thing for every level of nested transform. That means that any number of nested transforms

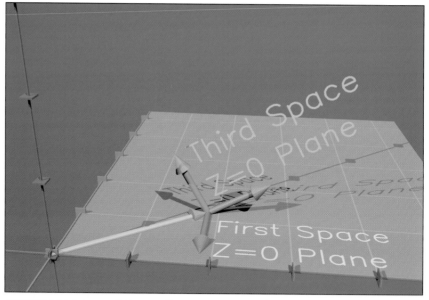

FIGURE 4.11 Intermediate coordinate space removed.
This is the same as Figure 4.10 with the intermediate second coordinate space removed. The vectors defining the third space in terms of the second were transformed to the first space. They now define the third space directly in terms of the first. With this trick, we can remove any number of intermediate coordinate spaces to go straight from one space to any other. This guarantees that we never have to store more than four vectors to define a 3D transform, regardless of how convoluted the transform was as originally defined.

can always be collapsed into one single equivalent transform. That's really handy, because we never need more than 12 numbers to store a transform, regardless of the original messy process used to derive it.

Unnatural Acts

So far I've shown you only rather tame 3D transforms. You've already seen examples of translation (moving to a different place) and rotation (changing the orientation in some way). The images in Figures 4.12 through 4.17 show you the full gamut of what's possible. Think of a transform as a combination of displacement, scaling, rotation, and skewing. However, keep in mind that no matter how many unnatural acts are combined, the result can still be described by a displacement vector and three basis vectors.

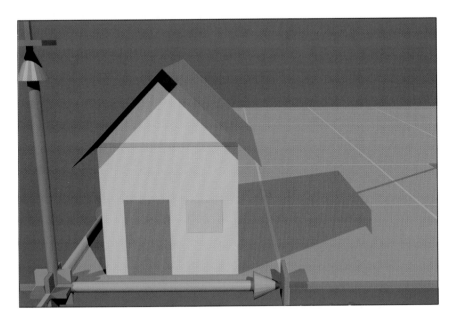

FIGURE 4.12 Object in original position.

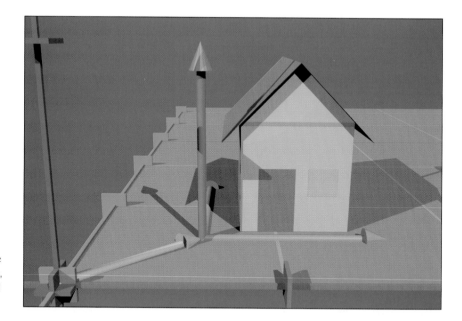

FIGURE 4.13
Displacement only.
The object's coordinate system is displaced (0.6, 0.5, 0) from the original position.

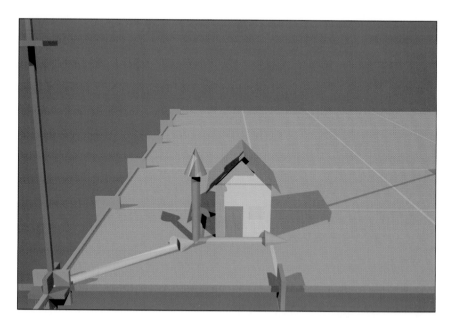

FIGURE 4.14
Displacement and scaling.
All three basis vectors are scaled by ½.

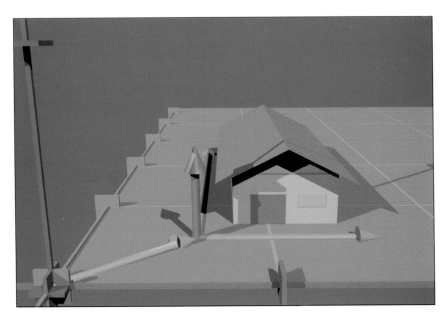

**FIGURE 4.15
Displacement and non-uniform scaling.**
The *Y* basis vector (green) is scaled by 2, while the *Z* basis vector (blue) is scaled by ½.

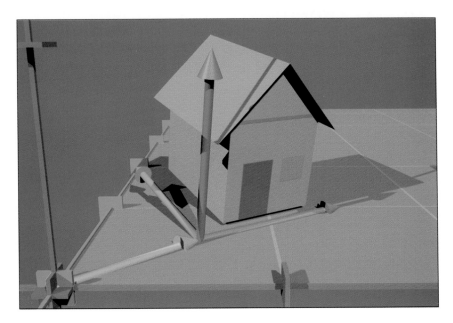

**FIGURE 4.16
Displacement and rotation.**
The object's coordinate system was first rotated 30° about its *Z* axis, then 10° about its *X* axis.

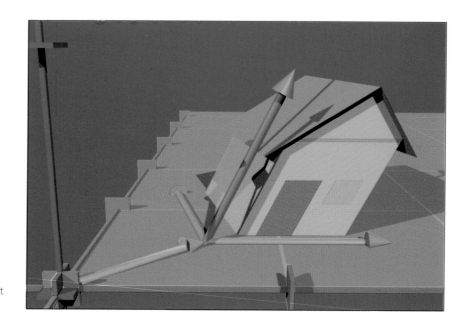

FIGURE 4.17
Displacement and
skewing.
Skewing results when
the X, Y and Z basis
vectors do not meet at
right angles.

4 × 4 HOMOGENEOUS TRANSFORMS

You may sometimes hear of **4 × 4** or **homogeneous transforms**. These can do everything one of our 4 × 3 transforms can do, plus more. Unfortunately, you can't make sense of the individual numbers in a 4 × 4 homogeneous transform the way we did with 4 × 3 transforms. Homogeneous transforms really are too complicated for this book. Fortunately, you can use a homogeneous transform like a regular 4 × 3 by filling in 0s and 1s in the right places. You almost never need the extra flexibility that 4 × 4 transforms provide. When graphics systems use them, they usually do so more for internal reasons than to provide additional features. This is the only place in this book where homogeneous transforms are even mentioned.

5

Modeling

WHAT IS MODELING?

No, computers don't walk down runways wearing the latest designer fashions, although they do sometimes get their photos on magazine covers. In computer graphics, **modeling** is the process of describing an object or scene so that we can eventually draw it. Because the resulting description, or model, is primarily intended for making pictures, we try to model things in a way that makes them easy to draw. A computer graphics model of a bridge might be quite different from the engineering model of the same bridge used for calculating stresses, deflections, and more.

Although modeling can encompass everything in a scene, including lights and the camera, this chapter is only about modeling the objects themselves (that's plenty for one chapter). In Chapter 6, "The Whole Scene (Lights, Camera, Action!)", we'll get into the rest of that stuff.

MODEL TYPES

As you might imagine, programmers have contrived lots of different schemes to explain graphics objects to a computer. I'll introduce you to the most common ones and their associated buzzwords.

Explicit Surfaces

Most objects in the real world are opaque, meaning we can see only their surfaces. If all we can see is the surface of an object, can we get away with describing only this surface? Isn't the picture of a closed opaque box the same whether it contains pirate gold, the meat loaf from last winter, or nothing at all?

Yes, yes, and yes again! This realization is the basis for the vast majority of computer graphics modeling.

Surfaces are often easier to describe than volumes, but there's another important advantage. The vast majority of 3D rendering hardware can draw only surfaces anyway. One rendering method, ray tracing, inherently handles volumes, but ray tracers are still essentially software-only. (We'll get into ray tracing in Chapter 7, "Rendering.")

An **explicit surface** model is one where an outright list is supplied of all the surface elements, or patches, that make up a surface.

Polygons   The predominant method for modeling surfaces is with polygons. (For a refresher on polygons, see page 34.) Many objects have flat surfaces with straight edges. These can be modeled with polygons directly.

Curved surfaces, however, are a greater challenge. A curved surface is broken into a set of abutting polygons, usually triangles or quadrilaterals. This process is called **tessellation**. Breaking up the surface into lots of small polygons models the surface more closely than using a small numbers of large polygons. Of course, large numbers of polygons take more memory, processing time, and drawing time. The relative "fineness" of the model is often called the **tessellation level**. Figure 5.1 shows the same object modeled at two different tessellation levels.

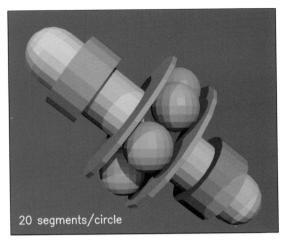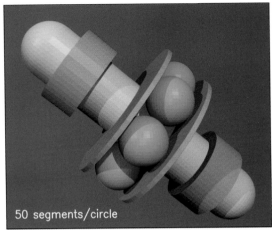

20 segments/circle

50 segments/circle

FIGURE 5.1 Polygonal model of curved surfaces.
The same object was modeled with polygons at a low tessellation level on the left, and a higher tessellation level on the right. The segments/circle values indicate the minimum number of line segments used to approximate a whole circle.

I don't want to give you the impression that all polygonal models need to look faceted, meaning they look composed of flat panels, or facets. We can apply some rendering (not modeling) tricks to make them look smooth. We'll get into the details later when we talk about shading in Chapter 7 on page 113. For now, just take a look at Figure 5.2 to convince yourself that it can be done.

Curved Patches   Several mathematical functions conveniently describe particular types of curved surfaces. Unfortunately, we're usually not interested in drawing any of these mathematical surfaces. The solution is to model small regions, or patches, of our curved surface with patches of the convenient mathematical functions. This is the same concept as tessellating the surface into polygons, except that we're using curved patches instead of polygons. The advantage is that we can get a closer fit to the intended surface with fewer patches.

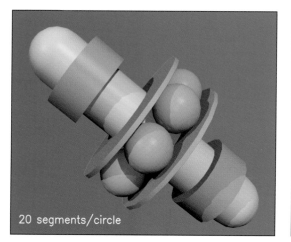
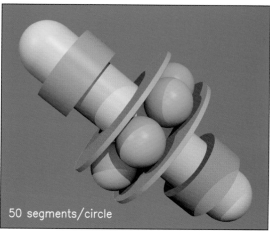

20 segments/circle   50 segments/circle

FIGURE 5.2 Polygonal model with smooth surface rendering.
Images drawn from polygonal models don't have to look faceted. These images are from the same models as in Figure 5.1 with a "smooth shading" rendering trick applied to them. The details of this are discussed in the "What Color Is the Object at This Pixel?" section of Chapter 7, starting on page 112.

Few rendering methods and almost no 3D graphics hardware can draw these curved patches directly, so they will eventually be decomposed into polygons. Why not use polygons directly? The model is often more compact and accurate with curved patches, and producing polygons from the patches is relatively little work. Because the polygon tessellation level is not dictated by the model, one model can be used to make both quick-and-dirty and slow-and-accurate pictures.

The mathematical details of curved patches are beyond the scope of this book. Some common types you might hear about are called **biquadratic** or **bicubic** patches.

Spline Patches   A **spline patch** is a curved patch where the mathematical function is governed by a set of **control points**. The patch takes on a smooth shape based on the position of these control points. Figure 5.3 shows an example of this where the resulting patch passed through the control points.

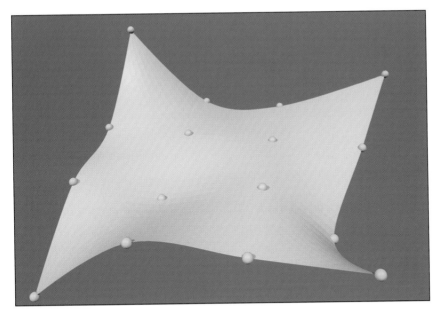

FIGURE 5.3 3D splined patch.
This patch was created by splining 16 control points, shown as yellow spheres. There are lots of different methods for creating a patch from a set of control points. Often, the patch doesn't pass through the control points as it does in this example.

There are many different mathematical formulas for creating a smooth surface from a set of control points. They vary in the mathematical properties of the resulting patch and how "loosely" or "tightly" the control points are followed. The details of all the different methods are beyond the scope of this book. Some common types you might hear about are **NURBS** (nonuniform rational b-splines), **B-splines**, and **beta splines**, although there are quite a few others.

Implicit Surfaces

An **implicit surface** is described by a mathematical function that can answer whether any point you ask about is to one side, to the other side, or on a surface. For many surface types, mathematical functions that do this can be much simpler than ones that explicitly provide a list of surface points. The downside is that eventually surface points will have to be found so that the surface can be drawn.

There are lots of different implicit surface types. I'll show you two types just to give you a better feel for what implicit surfaces are. I wouldn't bother trying to remember the details, just the general flavor.

Isosurfaces   An **isosurface** is where a value in a volume is at a particular threshold. *Iso-* means "at a constant value." You can think of isosurfaces as 2D contour lines extended to 3D. See Figure 5.4 as an example.

Potential Functions   Suppose you had a mathematical function that gave you a value depending on how close you were to a particular point. The value might be 1 when you're right on top of the point and fall off to 0 as you get farther and farther away. You could define an implicit surface as anywhere the closeness function was $\frac{1}{2}$, for example. In that case, the surface would be just a sphere. But now think about having a bunch of these points, each with its own closeness

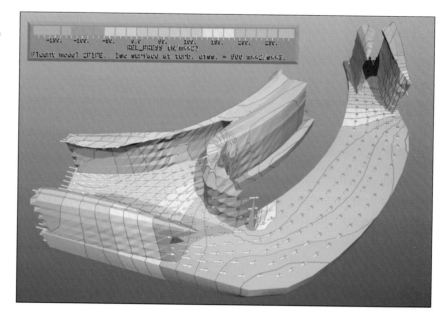

FIGURE 5.4 Isosurface example.
This image is a visualization of gas flow. The gas enters at the left and splits into the two pipes at the top. The pipes were cut open halfway up, and an isosurface was used to show where the gas had a particular turbulent energy dissipation. The isosurfaces form the irregular shapes that stick up from the sliced open pipes.
Numerical data courtesy of Fluent, Inc.

function. You could define a more interesting surface as anywhere the *sum* of all the closeness functions was $\frac{1}{2}$, for example. You can play with the number and arrangements of the points, their relative "strengths" (how fast the closeness function falls off to 0), and the cutoff value at which the surface is defined to model a variety of shapes.

Visually, this method builds surfaces by melding lots of little blobs together. The blobs are spheres when far apart, and they bleed into each other when close together, as shown in Figure 5.5. The potential function modeling method is sometimes referred to as modeling with **blobbies**. The term **potential function** refers to the mathematical functions that decrease as you get farther away from an object. It's possible to do this with other objects such as cones and cylinders, but points are definitely the easiest to work with. (See Figures 5.6 and 5.7 for examples of potential functions.)

Constructive Solid Geometry (CSG)

Constructive solid geometry models whole objects, not just their surfaces. Objects are created by combining simple 3D

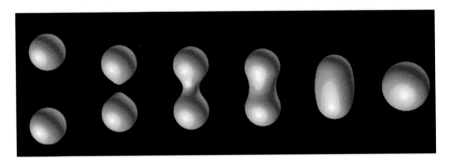

FIGURE 5.5 Potential function of two points.
This image shows six different objects, each modeled with two potential functions, or blobs. When far apart, the blobs don't interact much, leaving two spheres. Note how they smoothly blend together to form one surface when sufficiently close.
Image by Brian Wyvill, Computer Science Department, University of Calgary.

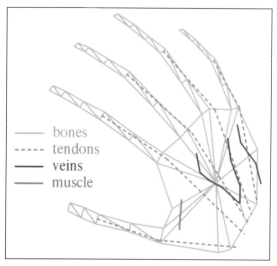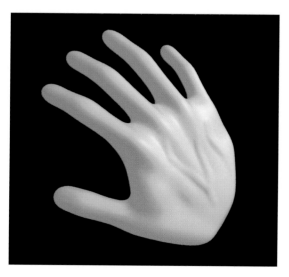

—— bones
----- tendons
—— veins
—— muscle

FIGURE 5.6 Potential function example.
This example illustrates how a smooth, complex object can be modeled with relatively few potential functions. If any of the joints are flexed in the schematic on the left, the outer skin surface on the right would follow in a reasonable way without requiring any additional work.
© 1991, Jules Bloomenthal.

solids using only three basic operators. These are sometimes referred to as **Boolean operators**.

The simple 3D solids are usually objects such as spheres, boxes, cones, and cylinders. The complexity and number of these solids depends on the particular CSG software.

The basic operators are often called **OR**, **AND**, and **NOT**, although they sometimes go by other names. Instead of giving the rigorous definition of these operators, see the 2D examples in Figures 5.8 through 5.10. At the level of this book, it's not important that you remember exactly what these operators do, but rather the general flavor of how CSG builds complex shapes from simple shapes and operators.

Unfortunately the names of the CSG operators aren't standard. The OR operator is also called **UNION**, and AND may be called **INTERSECTION**. Box AND NOT disc may

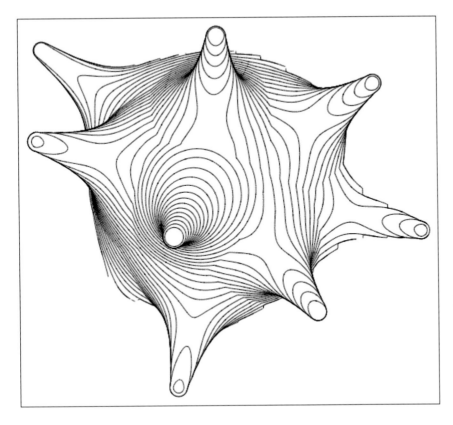

FIGURE 5.7 Potential function example.
This object was modeled with potential functions, but drawn with contour lines instead of surface patches.
© 1991, Jules Bloomenthal.

sometimes be referred to as box **MINUS** disc. **EXCLUSIVE OR** is often called just **XOR**.

The real power of CSG comes from combining multiple operations to produce complex shapes. Figure 5.11 is a simple example where three objects were subtracted from a cube. Figure 5.12 is an example where CSG was used to model a real object.

Space Subdivision

In **space subdivision modeling**, you don't describe the objects directly, but instead describe what's found in various regions, or subdivisions, of space. This is the same concept as using

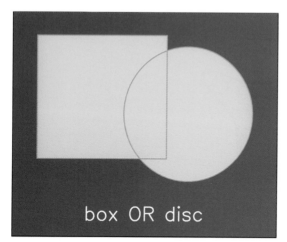
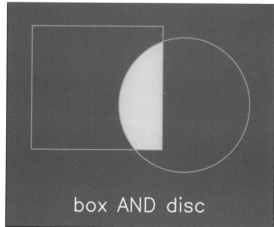

FIGURE 5.8 CSG OR and AND operators.
The OR operator simply combines both objects. In other words, the resulting object is present wherever either of the original objects were present. The AND operator produces an object only where both of the original objects were present.

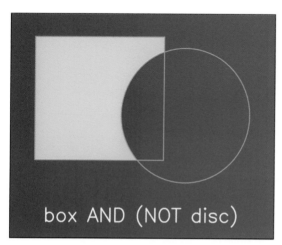
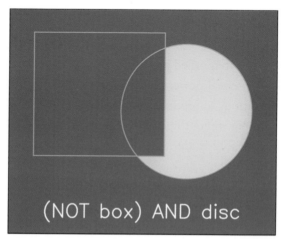

FIGURE 5.9 CSG "cutout" operations.
The NOT operator produces an object only where the original object was not present. ANDing with the NOT of an object is like using that object to make a cutout.

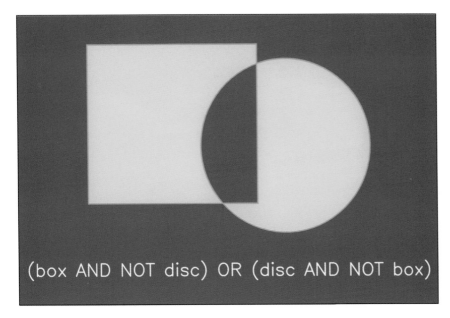

(box AND NOT disc) OR (disc AND NOT box)

FIGURE 5.10 CSG EXCLUSIVE OR operation.
The simple AND, OR, and NOT operators can be combined to achieve more complicated operations. This particular operation is called EXCLUSIVE OR and is sometimes included in the basic set of CSG operators.

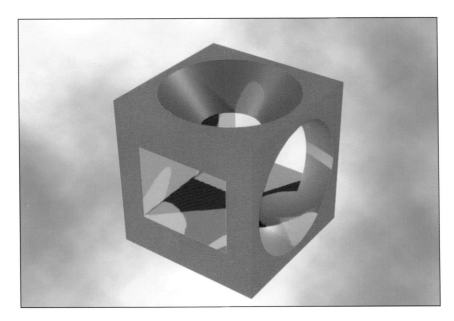

FIGURE 5.11 Simple CSG example.
Created using TriSpectives, courtesy 3D/EYE Inc.

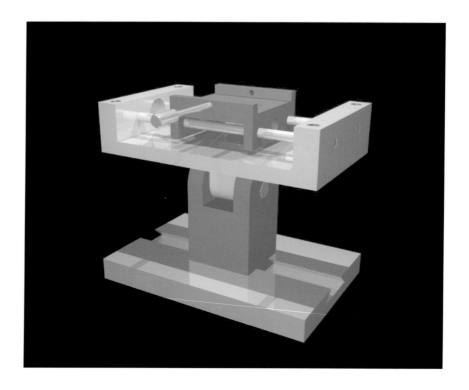

FIGURE 5.12 CSG example.

Courtesy Hewlett-Packard and 3D/EYE Inc.

pixels to describe a picture instead of the lines, points, and polygons used to draw that picture. In fact, the little regions of space are often called **voxels**, which comes from *volume elements.*

Of course, things are never that simple. We could just impose a regular 3D grid on an object, but that usually requires too much memory for useful resolutions. Consider a modest 2D image that has 500×500 pixels. That's only a quarter million pixels. But, a $500 \times 500 \times 500$ volume has 125 million voxels. Worse yet, the number of voxels goes up with the cube of the resolution. Doubling the resolution in each dimension to $1,000 \times 1,000 \times 1,000$ increases the number of voxels by eight, to 1 billion. Even if we had enough memory for 1 billion voxels, we'd still have to do at least a billion operations just to use the model.

The way we deal with both the size and speed issues is to not subdivide all the space at the same resolution. When you're modeling an opaque object, you don't need much information about its interior or the air around it. All the action is on the object's surface. In general, you don't need detailed information in any region of space that contains the same thing throughout, meaning it is **homogeneous**.

There are a number of techniques for exploiting homogeneity. I've picked the two that you're most likely to run into or hear about.

Octrees In octree modeling, the whole model starts out in one rectangular block. Blocks are broken up until either they are homogeneous or the desired resolution is achieved. Octree voxels are always rectangular solids, and they are always broken in the middle along each of the three major axes. This yields eight (that's where the *oct* in octree comes from) subblocks that have the same shape as the original block.

It's easier to show this concept in two dimensions where rectangles are split in four instead of boxes in eight. These structures are often called **quadtrees** (*quad* refers to four). Take a look at Figure 5.13.

Octrees are often used for storing 3D volumetric data. Each voxel is subdivided only if the data values within it aren't all the same. In addition, the largest and smallest data value within a voxel can be kept for every voxel in the octree. This speeds up finding all the places where the data is a particular value. For example, if you want to draw the surface where the data value is 59, you don't have to waste effort processing a voxel (and possibly a large number of subvoxels) that contains only data values from 13 to 43. See Figure 5.14.

Binary Space Subdivision (BSP) Trees In this method, if a block of space isn't homogeneous, it's broken into two blocks

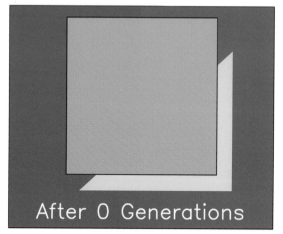

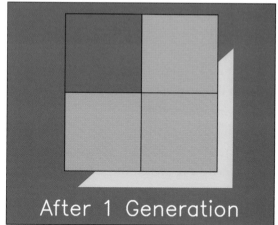

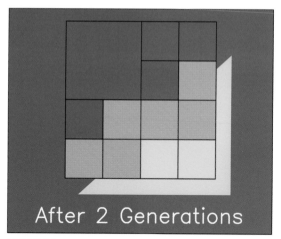

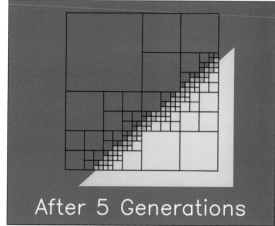

FIGURE 5.13 Quadtree examples.

Quadtrees are the 2D equivalents of 3D octrees. The yellow triangle and blue background are being modeled by the quadtree. Nonhomogeneous rectangles are gray. Note that only these rectangles are subdivided further. Most of the action is therefore concentrated on the object's edge.

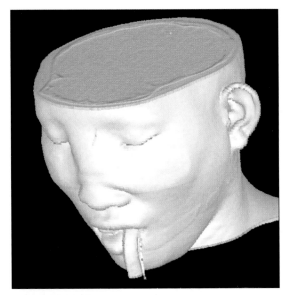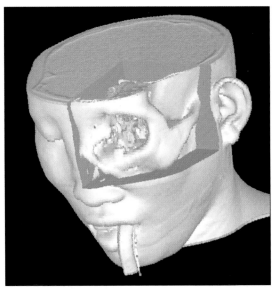

FIGURE 5.14 Octree examples.

These images are both from the same octree of a CT scan data set. The left image shows the volume where the data value indicated some tissue was present. The right image is the same, except that only the volume where the data indicated bone is shown in the cutaway region.

Images courtesy of Octree Corporation.

(hence the name *binary*). This process continues with each of the new blocks until either they are homogeneous or a resolution limit is reached.

There are several variations of this method that differ in how the blocks are subdivided. In **regular BSP trees,** the blocks are all rectangular solids, and they are subdivided exactly in half, parallel to one of the faces. This makes it easy to describe how each box was split because there are only three possible choices. On the other hand, blindly breaking a block in the middle is not the most efficient way to subdivide exactly where it's needed.

At the other extreme, blocks can be cut in two by an arbitrary plane. This will require less subdivision to reach the same model resolution. However, it's more difficult to describe each of the subdivisions, and the resulting blocks are more difficult to manipulate because they can have complicated shapes.

Procedural Models

Procedural models are described by a method, or procedure, for producing primitives when necessary instead of the primitives themselves.

Procedural models are often useful when the required level of detail isn't known when the model is created. The procedure can be performed later as necessary to achieve the desired level of detail. Procedural models may also be more compact than an explicit list of primitives.

Fractals   **Fractals** are functions that have infinite detail. Examples can be found in nature that exhibit similar "roughness" over wide ranges of magnification. For example, the shape of a coastline will have a similar look and feel whether you plot a 1,000-mile stretch every 10 miles, or a 1-mile stretch every $1/100$ mile.

Some mathematical functions are fractals. One example you might have bumped into is a **Mandelbrot set function**. Such a function produces a value given a 2D coordinate. In Figure 5.15, the different values from a Mandelbrot set function were drawn as different colors. The details of how a Mandelbrot set function works are beyond the scope of this book.

There are a number of procedures for creating fractal and fractal-like surfaces for use in computer graphics. The inner workings of these procedures are beyond the scope of this book. These procedures are useful for creating objects with a particular look and feel, as long as the details aren't important. For example, you can use fractal procedures for creating

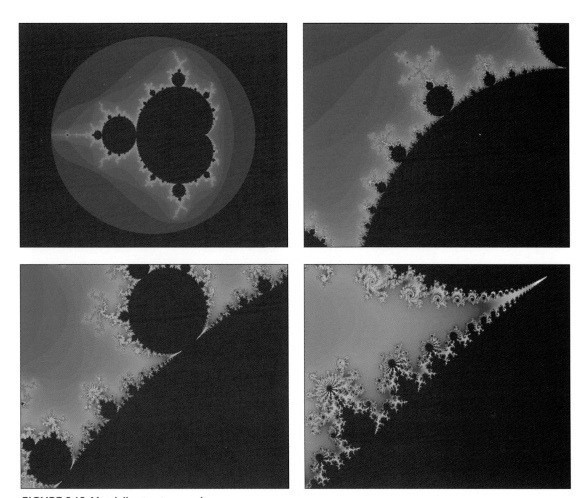

FIGURE 5.15 Mandelbrot set examples.
These four images show a Mandelbrot set at different magnification levels. The function never smooths out, regardless of how closely you look.
Images by Justin Ryan, class of 1996, and Brian DeRosa, class of 1997, Westford Academy, the public high school in Westford, Massachusetts.

convincing mountains, although you can't use them to model any one particular mountain. Take a look at Figure 5.16.

Graftals   You can loosely think of **graftals** as objects that are "grown" according to a strict recipe. I'm only going to get into this very superficially, because graftals aren't used that much.

FIGURE 5.16 Example including fractals.
This image shows a number of modeling techniques, including fractals. The rock on the left and the mountains in the background were created with a fractal-like procedure. This procedure includes some randomness, so it can't be used to model a particular mountain—the Matterhorn, for example. You can use it only to create shapes that generally look like mountains.

For example, you could model a bush by starting with the following recipe: "Make a short stick, then fork in two, then repeat this process for each of the two new sticks. After you've done this ten times, make a short stick that ends in a leaf." You could also include directions to "twist a little," "shrink," and so forth for each generation. (See Figure 5.17 for another graftal example.)

Particle Systems   In **particle system modeling,** the object is drawn as the tracks of large numbers of individual particles. Each particle has a start location and a trajectory. There might also be additional directions, like the particle's color along the trajectory.

FIGURE 5.17 Graftal example.
Image "green.flame", ©
1984, Alvy Ray Smith.

Particle systems are most useful when there are large numbers of particles that are only loosely controlled. You give general directions but let the computer use randomness for the details about each individual particle.

Particle systems have been used to create convincing pictures of waterfalls, fire, or a lawn full of grass blades. (See Figure 5.18, for example.)

OTHER MODELING ISSUES

So far we've talked only about the various ways of describing objects to a computer. This section deals with some other considerations that you should be aware of. I'll just mention them briefly.

Level of Detail

You should think about how detailed a model needs to be. More detailed models will result in more accurate and

FIGURE 5.18 Particle systems example.
The grass in this image was modeled with particle systems. Note how general direction was given about where the particles should originate to make the clumps of grass, the height, and the shape of the grass blades. Each individual particle, however, has randomly chosen specifics within the general rules. To model the flowers, spheres were drawn at the end of some of the particle trajectories.

realistic pictures, but they require more storage and computing resources, both to generate and to draw. The best trade-off depends on many factors, including the role the object plays in the final picture. Is the object large and the main focus of the image, or is it a minor part of the background? Take a look at Figure 5.19 to see some trade-offs in action.

All four combinations in Figure 5.19 may be appropriate, depending on the situation. In general, it makes sense to adjust the model detail depending on the final object size and importance. Note how the contrast between the coarse and fine models is more striking when the object is larger.

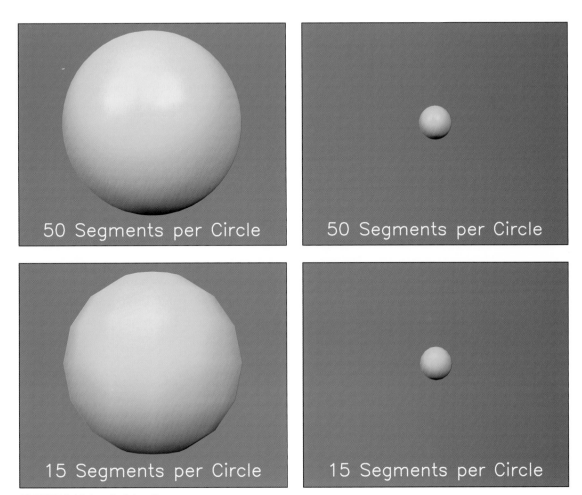

FIGURE 5.19 Level of detail.
The sphere is shown at two different sizes and differing model detail. The segments per circle value indicates the minimum number of line segments used to approximate a circle.

On the other hand, large and coarse can be useful for quick previews. The rough spheres in Figure 5.19 are modeled from fewer than 10 percent of the polygons as the finer spheres, which could significantly reduce their drawing time.

Small and detailed may also be appropriate. Suppose you need to make a high-resolution image for a poster. You know that people will be able to scrutinize its every detail. Also, computation may sometimes be free. Computers are often left on but idle during the night. You might as well use higher detail and have the machine finish at 7:00 in the morning instead of 8:00 at night, assuming there was nothing else for it to do.

Suitability for Other Purposes

Strange as it may seem, making computer-generated pictures may not be the only function of a model. Sometimes the choice of model type is dictated by these other functions.

For example, calculating surface area is easy with polygonal models, but very difficult with implicit surfaces. Other operations, such as milling and drilling, are easier to simulate with volumetric models. For those operations, CSG or octrees may be a better choice.

I don't want to get into this any further because it really isn't part of computer graphics. It's an issue that you should be aware of, though.

6

The Whole Scene (Lights, Camera, Action!)

So far we've talked about how to describe individual objects to a computer so it can draw their pictures. That's a bit like having actors, but no stage, lights, or audience. This chapter talks about the whole scene. A **scene** includes the objects and all the other stuff the computer needs to actually make a picture.

OBJECTS

The objects in a scene are what will ultimately get drawn. How these are described to the computer is what the previous chapter covered.

LIGHTS

Our brains get many subtle shape cues from how the brightness of an object varies across its surface. That we can recognize objects in black-and-white photographs is proof of how effective and automatic this mechanism is.

Brightness varies across an object's surface depending on how much it faces toward the predominant light. Your brain interprets these brightness variations into surface orientations and, ultimately, into three-dimensional shapes. Brightness can also vary because of the object's reflectivity and color. This can sometimes lead to shape confusion, but the brain is amazingly good at sorting it all out.

Shape perception works because light doesn't come from all directions equally. Our visual systems evolved under conditions where light came primarily from one relatively narrow direction: the sun. Even on a cloudy day, one part of the sky is usually brighter than the rest, and the sky is still only the upper half of our visual world. Sometimes the right combination of sunlight, clouds, and snow on the ground and in the air can cause a condition called *whiteout*. In a whiteout there is still plenty of light, but it is coming from all around. Whiteouts are known for their disorienting effect because they make features difficult to distinguish. The effect of lighting on shape perception is illustrated in Figure 6.1.

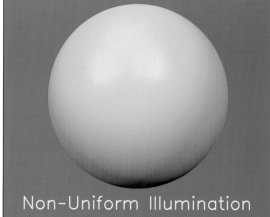

Uniform Illumination

Non-Uniform Illumination

FIGURE 6.1 Effect of lighting on shape perception.
These pictures illustrate how shape cues are derived from variations in object brightness as the surface curves toward or away from the light.

How Real Lights Work (As Opposed to How We're Going to Fudge It)

Before we talk about how the lighting environment is modeled in computer graphics, let's take a look at how real light works.

As you know intuitively, light gets dimmer as it gets farther away from its source. The exact relationship is that light intensity falls off with the square of the distance from the light source. This may be easier to remember and believe by looking at Figure 6.2.

Picture a light front leaving a point light source. The light travels with equal speed in all directions, so the front becomes an ever increasing sphere as it progresses. This light front contains a fixed amount of light energy, which is spread over larger and larger spheres. At 2 meters, this sphere has four times the square-meter surface area than at

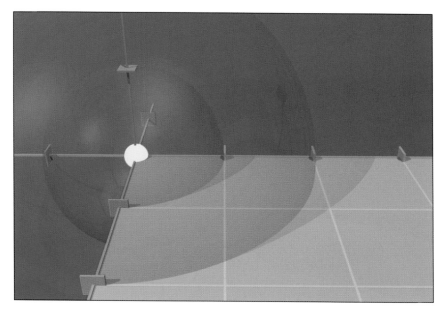

FIGURE 6.2 Light attenuating over distance.
Light is emitted from a light source indicated by the white ball. The two spheres show where the light energy is spread out at a distance of 1 and 2 units from the light source. The outer sphere has four times the surface area of the inner one, making the light four times as dim there.

1 meter. In fact, the surface area of a sphere is tied to the *square* of its radius. Because the light energy is spread out over the surface of a sphere, it diminishes by the square of the radius, or square of the distance to the light source. Even though the outer sphere in Figure 6.2 is only twice as far from the light, it has four times the surface area. A sphere at distance 3 would have nine (3^2) times the surface area, meaning the light would be nine times dimmer than at distance 1.

Surface orientation also affects how much light hits an object. We'll quantify how this works on page 115; for now, look at Figure 6.3 to get a feel for it.

Now that we've talked about how light really works, we'll look at how we model it in computer graphics. As you'll see, sometimes we can still get useful results while taking a few liberties with the physics.

FIGURE 6.3 Effect of surface angle on illumination.
This illustration shows three identical objects at different orientations to the light. The width of the shadow below each object shows how much light is hitting the object.

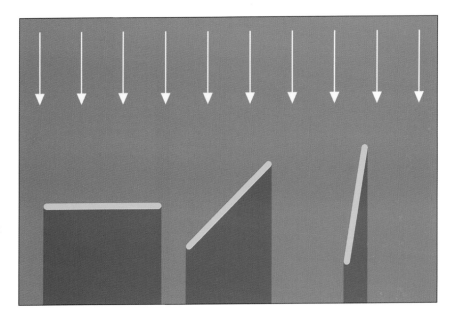

Directional Lights

As I mentioned, all light spreads out and gets dimmer as it gets farther from its source. Sometimes light sources are so far away that it's almost impossible to notice this on a human scale. Sunlight is a good example. Because it travels about 150 million kilometers (93 million miles) to get here, you won't likely notice that it gets .000013 percent dimmer in the 10 meters between the roof of your house and the ground.

Calculating light intensity due to distance from such a light source would be a waste of time. To save us the trouble, we use an expedient called a **directional light**. This kind of light is specified with only a direction to the light and an intensity, which apply everywhere in the scene.

Point Lights

A basic computer graphics **point light source** doesn't get dimmer with distance, but still comes from a point the way real light does. There is no way to justify this with physics. It's a commonly used convenience that decreases the computational requirements while still making believable and useful pictures in many cases.

A correct model for light is the **point light source with** $1/R^2$ **falloff**. Yes, it's a mouthful, but that's how it's commonly referred to. The R stands for *radius* and means the distance from the light source. In computer graphics, I would assume a point light source doesn't have any brightness falloff unless someone explicitly says so.

You may also encounter point lights that have some sort of brightness falloff, but not with the square of the distance from the light source. These are again computational conveniences that still often produce useful results.

Spotlights

A **spotlight** is intended to model a light that has some kind of shade or reflector around it so that it shines only in a cone. All spot lights have control over the cone angle. Some graphics systems also provide a region along the edge of the cone where the light can fall off gradually.

Ambient Light

Computer graphics **ambient light** is another convenient hack. It attempts to model the light that is scattered about by bouncing off other objects. For example, the floor under your desk doesn't appear completely black, even though no light source is shining on it directly. It is illuminated by light that's scattered by other objects, such as the wall and the bookcase.

Most rendering methods don't handle scattered light. (One exception is radiosity, but we'll get into that on page 109.) To make do, we pretend there's a constant low-level illumination everywhere, called *ambient light*. Because it's constant, it doesn't help with shape perception, but it does prevent areas from appearing completely black.

VIEW POINT (CAMERA)

Even if we have a nice definition of all the objects and lights in a scene, we still have to know where we're looking from, what we're looking directly at (or which direction we're looking in), and which way is supposed to be up in the final picture.

The point to look from is usually called the **eye point, view point,** or **camera point.** The direction to look into is called the **view direction** or **gaze direction.** A point that is to appear in the center of the picture is sometimes called the **lookat point**. The camera orientation about the gaze direction is usually specified by supplying an **up vector** or sometimes a **right** or **left vector**.

Beyond this, keep in mind that we're starting with a rich 3D definition and ultimately squishing the information onto a 2D image. Going from 3D to 2D involves throwing out some information. These are called **projection methods** (we're projecting a 3D scene onto a 2D image). As you might expect, there's no one right way of doing this. I've included the two that cover all but very specialized applications.

Perspective Projection

If I asked you to sketch a picture of your house, you'd probably draw it in perspective projection without thinking about it. In **perspective projection**, distant objects are drawn smaller than near ones. This is also how a camera works. Perspective projection results in what you would probably think of as a "normal" 3D picture.

To understand this geometrically, think of hanging a glass pane in front of your eye so that it frames the picture you want to draw. Now just draw right on the glass whatever you see behind it. The picture on the glass would be in perspective.

Another way of saying this is that all objects get projected onto the image along a line from the eye point, as is shown in Figure 6.4. Note how objects are drawn bigger as they get closer to the eye point.

Flat Projection

In **flat projection**, objects are projected flat onto the image without any change in size. This is also called

FIGURE 6.4 Perspective projection diagram.
This diagram shows how all objects are projected onto the image plane along a line from the eye point. The image plane is the transparent sheet, the eye point is the yellow ball, and the yellow arrows show how each object is projected onto the image plane. The two white stick figures on either side of the image plane are the same size. Note how the one in front is enlarged by the projection (shown in black), while the one in back is reduced.

**FIGURE 6.5
Orthographic
projection diagram.**
In orthographic, or flat, projection, objects are projected directly onto the image plane without any change in size. Note that orthographic projection is the same as perspective projection with the eye point infinitely far back.

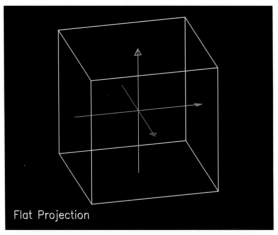
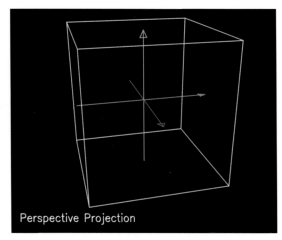

Flat Projection

Perspective Projection

FIGURE 6.6 Flat and perspective projection examples.
The outline of the cube is shown with flat projection on the left and perspective projection on the right. Note how you can't tell whether you are looking down or up at the left cube, while it's quite clear for the right cube. This is because our brains naturally interpret depth from the perspective projection scaling.

orthographic projection. Orthographic projection is used mainly where preserving dimensions is important, as on a mechanical drawing. Scale is then constant for the whole drawing—1 centimeter represents 3 meters, 1 palm equals 1 furlong, or whatever. (See Figures 6.5 and 6.6 for some examples.)

7

Rendering (Converting a Scene to Pixels)

WHAT IS RENDERING?

Rendering is the "drawing" part of computer graphics. It's the process of converting all the stuff in a scene into that 2D grid of pixels we call an image.

COMMON RENDERING METHODS

All sorts of rendering methods have been devised. Each one of them has its own advantages and disadvantages. I've chosen four methods that cover most of the mainstream applications: wire frame, Z buffer, ray tracing, and radiosity.

Wire-Frame Rendering

In **wire-frame rendering** only the edges of objects are drawn. You can think of this a bit like stick-figure drawing. If an object is modeled with polygons, we usually draw the edges of all the polygons. Figures 7.1 and 7.2 are examples of wire-frame rendering. Yes, this concept is really as simple as it looks.

Especially in Figure 7.2, it's a bit hard to see what's going on. So why would anyone use wire-frame rendering? Today the answer is mostly that wire frame can be faster and

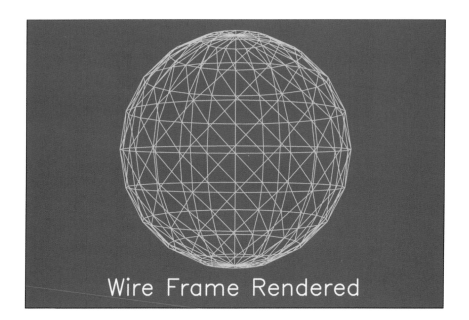

FIGURE 7.1 Wire-frame rendering example.

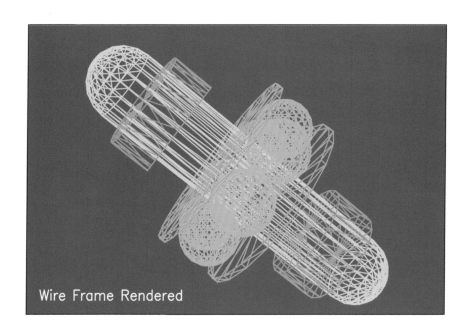

FIGURE 7.2 Wire-frame rendering example.

therefore useful for quick previews. If you just wanted to see how the image was framed, Figure 7.2 would do the job. Wire frame is often faster because today's common display controllers (page 22) can draw lines in hardware, whereas reasonable-looking solid objects require significant software intervention.

For certain applications, wire frame makes the most sense, regardless of speed. Some mechanical drawings, for example, are clearer when only the edges of objects are drawn.

As solid rendering hardware becomes more common, wire frame will be used only where drawing lines is inherently better than drawing solid surfaces. Now that single chip solid rendering display controllers are becoming available, there will be very little price advantage to hardware that can draw only lines. High-end PC systems are coming standard with solid rendering hardware in 1996, and will be standard in virtually all PC systems by late 1997.

Back in neolithic times (up to about the late 1980s), there were other reasons for wire-frame rendering. Some hardware could draw only lines, not fill in areas. Printers were for text, and graphics output was made on plotters. Plotters worked on the principle of dragging a scribe across a clay tablet, although the scribe was usually a felt-tipped pen and the tablet had become a sheet of paper. Very early display controllers, called **calligraphic controllers**, didn't have a bitmap of pixels. They used a completely different method that could only draw lines on the screen.

Z-Buffer Rendering

What would happen if we simply drew every polygon of a scene into the bitmap? We'd have solid surface rendering, right? Well, it probably wouldn't look like what you were expecting. Remember that objects are usually modeled without regard to the direction from which you look at them. That means the model contains all the polygons of an object, including the ones on the back side. The final picture, however, must come from only those polygons that we actually see. A polygon might be invisible because it's on the back side of an object or because it's occluded (the view of it is blocked) by another object. To make things even more difficult, a polygon may be partially visible.

In **Z-buffer rendering**, only the unoccluded surfaces are drawn. This is done by maintaining an additional value in each bitmap pixel beyond the color. This value is referred to as the **Z value**. The Z values for all the pixels in a bitmap are referred to as the **Z buffer**. A Z value is a measure of the distance from the eye point to the point on the object represented by the pixel where the Z value is stored.

Before any polygons are drawn, all the Z values are set to indicate the farthest distance from the eye they can represent. All the polygons are then drawn, which may result in some pixels being hit more than once. Before a new value is written into a pixel, the pixel's Z value is compared to the new Z value. If the new Z value represents a closer distance to the eye point, the new value is written into the pixel. Otherwise, the pixel is left alone. After all the polygons are drawn, each pixel is left with the value from the frontmost surface of the frontmost object.

In Figures 7.3 and 7.4 we'll walk through an example where two triangles are written into a small bitmap using the Z-buffer algorithm. The triangles intersect, and we will end up with only those parts of the triangles that are not occluded.

Two important properties of Z-buffer rendering are worth remembering. First, note that we could have drawn the two triangles in reverse order and still ended up with the

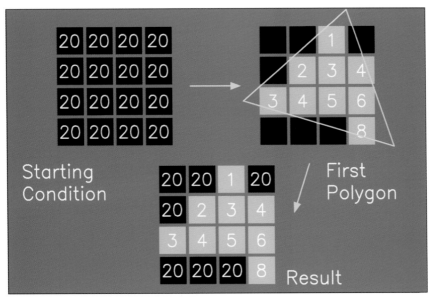

FIGURE 7.3 Z-buffer diagram 1.
Before rendering is started, the pixel colors are set to the background color, and the Z values are set to the value that represents the maximum distance. In this example, the background color is black, and Z values range from 0 to 20, with larger numbers representing greater distances. The pixel colors are shown directly, and the Z values are shown as numbers.

 The top left bitmap shows the initial conditions. The colors are all black (background), and the Z values are all 20 (maximum distance). The first triangle is drawn into the bitmap at top right. For each pixel, the triangle's Z value is compared to the Z value in the bitmap. The triangle is drawn into a pixel only if the new Z value represents a closer distance (lower number in this example) than the Z value already in the pixel. In this example, the entire triangle is closer than the maximum distance, so all its pixels are drawn.

same result. Z buffers are order-independent. (Well, almost order-independent. In case of a tie you have to make an arbitrary choice as to whether to take the old or the new value, but this rarely matters in practice.)

 The second important property of Z-buffer rendering is that it can be done incrementally. Note that Figure 7.4 started with only the final result from Figure 7.3. We didn't have to know about previously rendered polygons to render more

FIGURE 7.4 Z-buffer diagram 2.
We now start with the result from Figure 7.3. The magenta triangle is drawn into the bitmap using the Z-buffer algorithm. This time some of the new triangle's Z values are greater than the ones already in the bitmap. Note that the pixels where this is the case are not altered. The resulting bitmap contains the color values from only the closest surface for each pixel.

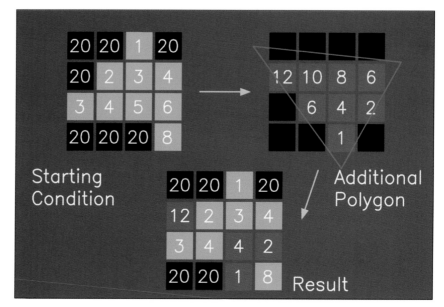

polygons. All we need is the resulting bitmap, no matter how it was derived.

We should also talk a little about how the Z, or depth, value is represented. In the example, I used values from 0 to 20. In practice, you need many more depth values to accurately determine what's in front of what. Z values are usually stored in 16 bits, which results in about 66,000 different depth values. That's usually quite adequate if the front and back limits of the Z buffer in the scene are chosen with a little care. Some early Z-buffer systems used only 12 bits for Z, yielding about 4,000 depth values. The images these systems produced often suffered from artifacts due to the low Z resolution—for example, ragged intersection edges. Today's systems all use at least 16 bits for the Z value. All the Z-buffered images in this book were rendered using 16-bit Z values.

Imagine rendering a picture of a car using 16-bit Z values. For the sake of example, let's say you need a 16-foot range to include the whole car. This means you've got about

66,000 depth values spread over 16 feet. The average distance between adjacent depth values is about 75 micrometers, or about half the thickness of many bumper stickers. Typical office paper is 80 to 100 micrometers thick.

Z buffering is the most common solid surface rendering technique today. It is simple enough to be implemented directly in inexpensive hardware. In fact, most of the cost in adding Z buffering to a display controller is the memory for all the bitmap Z values (the Z buffer). This same simplicity also makes software implementations fast compared to the other solid rendering methods we'll talk about. In mid-1996, $2,000 to $4,000 desktop systems can render three to ten thousand 100-pixel Z-buffered triangles per second in software. Systems with hardware Z buffers are about 100 times faster.

While Z buffering does a good job rendering the correct visible surfaces, it doesn't address how light interacts between objects at all. Take a good look at the examples in Figures 7.5 and 7.6 to get a feel for what Z-buffered pictures look like.

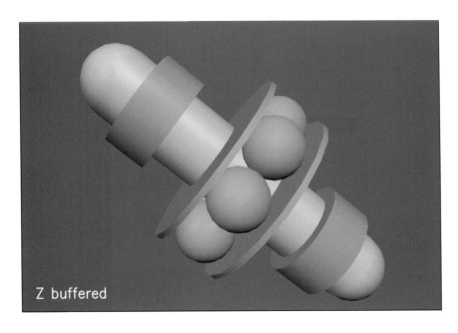

Z buffered

FIGURE 7.5 Example of Z-buffer rendering.

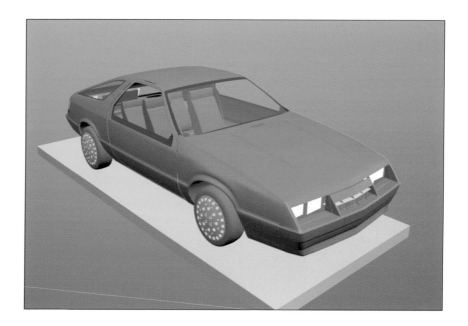

**FIGURE 7.6 Example
of Z-buffer rendering.**
*Data courtesy of Chrysler
Corporation.*

Ray Tracing

In Z buffering, we render one object at a time until we run
out of objects. We might access any of the bitmap pixels for
each object.

In ray tracing, we render one pixel at a time until we run
out of pixels. We might access any of the objects for each
bitmap pixel.

Figure 7.7 shows the basic concept behind **ray tracing**.
For each pixel, a ray is shot from the eye point in the view
direction for that pixel. The pixel is then set to the color of
whatever the ray bumps into.

Here's another way to think of ray tracing: Imagine you
are following the light for a pixel backward to see what color
it is. Note that this process doesn't stop when the first object
is encountered. Unless the object is a light source, the light
from that spot on the object came from somewhere else.
With ray tracing, we can follow several possible sources of

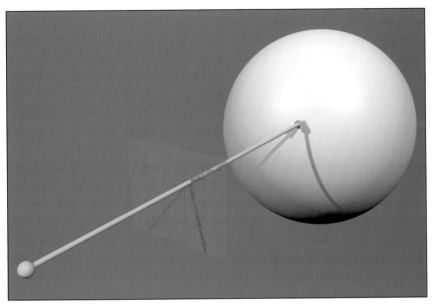

FIGURE 7.7 Ray-tracing basic concept.
When ray tracing, you can think of the bitmap as hanging a short distance in front of the eye point. The eye point is shown here as the small yellow sphere, and the bitmap pixels as the grid of semitransparent squares. The only object in this example scene is the large white sphere. To find out what color a pixel is, you shoot a ray from the eye point through the pixel. The pixel color comes from whatever point on whatever object the ray bumps into. If the ray doesn't hit anything, the pixel is set to the background color.

that light to find out what color *they* are. This is done by shooting more rays, one in each direction where light might be coming from. These rays, in turn, may cause even more rays to be launched. This process of determining a ray's color by launching more rays is called **recursive ray tracing,** as diagrammed in Figure 7.8. This method is so common that it's generally assumed to be the method used when people say just "ray tracing." Some people say **ray casting** to denote nonrecursive ray tracing, but I think that's too much splitting of hairs.

In theory, some rays might keep launching more rays indefinitely. This could happen where there are lots of

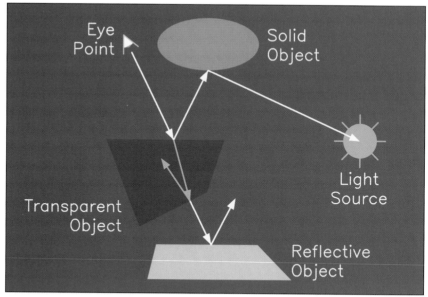

FIGURE 7.8 Recursive ray-tracing diagram.
This diagram shows how many rays may be launched in an effort to resolve the color of one pixel. The original ray, often called an *eye ray,* starts at the eye point at top left. Additional rays are launched when a reflective or transparent object is hit, and to determine whether a point is illuminated by a light source. Refraction effects are modeled when rays are followed into and back out of transparent objects. Shadows result when a ray toward a light source, often called a *light ray,* hits something else before getting to the light source. If the transparent and reflective objects had not been purely transparent and reflective (as if they were coated with dust, for example), light rays would have been launched from them, too.

reflective objects in a scene, for example. In practice, new rays are not launched when their importance to the original pixel color is small enough to ignore, or when an arbitrary recursion limit is reached. Typical cutoff values are between five and ten recursive generations. Without some sort of limit, the computer could spend way too long on just one pixel.

Now it's time to get a feel for what this looks like in practice, so see Figures 7.9 through 7.11. Note that unlike Z-buffered images, ray-traced images can have shadows and reflections. Shadows in particular seem to help the human

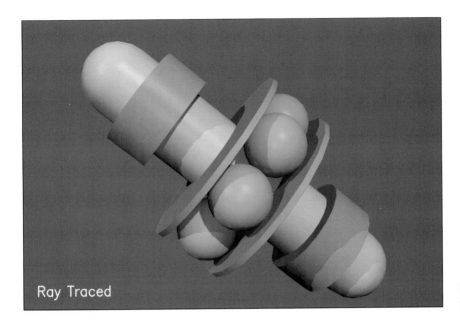

Ray Traced

FIGURE 7.9 Ray-tracing example.

FIGURE 7.10 Ray-tracing example.

Data courtesy of Chrysler Corporation.

FIGURE 7.11 Ray-tracing example.
*Rendered by Eric Haines.
© 1988, Hewlett-Packard
Company.*

visual system understand the relative positions of objects. This is particularly evident by comparing Figures 7.10 and 7.6.

Speed Issues   Ray tracing has a reputation of being a slow way to render pictures. It's no good in real-time situations, unless you happen to be studying plant growth or plate tectonics.

Ray tracing is relatively slow for two main reasons. First, the algorithm is more complex than other methods and has therefore not been implemented in generally available hardware. Second, it does its work per pixel instead of per object. For most of today's scenes, pixels greatly outnumber objects. It helps to understand the Z-buffer and ray-tracing algorithms by thinking about their relative speeds.

A Z-buffer renderer visits each polygon once, although it may draw any pixel several times. In hardware Z-buffer systems, the hardware usually does the per-pixel work, while the software feeds polygons to the hardware. Except for very large polygons (which therefore require the hardware to draw lots of pixels) the bottleneck is the software. This means a Z buffer's speed depends mostly on the number of polygons it has to draw.

A ray tracer, by contrast, draws each pixel exactly once, although it may visit some primitives many times and others not at all. It's been shown that ray tracers that use the space subdivision speedup method (we'll get into that on page 108) don't slow down much as the number of objects increases. (The exact reasons for this are beyond the scope of this book, but it has something to do with front objects occluding ever more back objects.) A ray tracer's speed is therefore mostly dependent on the number of pixels in the image.

For a fixed-size bitmap, a Z buffer slows down more quickly than a ray tracer as objects are added to the scene. This implies that ray tracing may actually be faster for images of very complex scenes. This is, in fact, true. However, for most of today's scenes and bitmaps, Z buffers are significantly faster.

Consider the ray tracer's task in rendering Figure 7.12. The image size is 2,048 × 1,366 pixels. The scene contains 300 reflective spheres illuminated by two directional light sources.

To render the top left pixel, the ray tracer would first need to do a few calculations, including a square root, to get the starting ray from the eye point. It then has to find the data for sphere 1 and perform a ray/sphere intersection check. This takes a few more calculations, after which it determines that the ray doesn't intersect sphere 1. It can now forget about

FIGURE 7.12 Ray-tracing a complex scene.
Ray traced image of 300 reflective spheres illuminated by two directional lights and an ambient light.

sphere 1, so it's on to spheres 2, 3, 4, and on and on until it finally finishes with sphere 300. It now knows the ray doesn't hit any object in the scene and sets the pixel to the blue background color. All that's left to do now are the remaining 2,797,567 pixels.

And what happens when a ray does hit a sphere? Then there's some real work to do. One ray is launched to each of the two light sources to find whether the spot on the sphere is directly illuminated. Because the sphere is reflective (as defined in the model), a new ray is also launched in the direction from which the reflected light came. This new ray now has to be checked against spheres 1, 2, ...

By now you're probably wondering how Figure 7.12 was rendered in your lifetime, let alone Figure 7.13, which contains 1,100 spheres. It certainly wasn't done with the basic brute-force algorithm I've described. The basic algorithm was modified to make it much faster. All ray tracers use some sort

FIGURE 7.13 Another complex ray-traced image.
This ray-traced picture of a DNA molecule contains 1,100 spheres.

of speedup technique. These come in two basic flavors, called *object hierarchy* and *space subdivision*. We'll discuss both of these, because the speedup technique is an important part of a ray tracer.

In **object hierarchy ray tracing**, clumps of objects are collected into groups, then clumps of groups are collected into bigger groups, and so on. For each group, a simple shape such as a sphere or a box is found that's as small as reasonably possible yet still contain everything in the group. This is often called the **bounding volume**. Instead of checking a ray against every object in the group, the ray is checked against the bounding volume first. If it doesn't intersect the bounding volume, then there's no need to go any further with any object or subgroup in the group.

Object hierarchy ray tracing can be quite effective, especially if objects naturally form into nice clusters. Much of the performance hinges on how the groups are selected, which is difficult to do well automatically with arbitrary scenes. Partially for this reason, most general-purpose ray tracers don't use object hierarchies as the main speedup tactic.

Space subdivision ray tracers also seek to easily eliminate fruitless ray/object intersection checks, but they do so with a completely different approach. The scene space is subdivided into little regions. Each region contains a list of the objects found within that region. Rays are traced from their start points through each of the regions in their path. Intersection checks are performed only on objects listed in the regions.

There are many schemes for subdividing the scene space. One method simply divides it into $32 \times 32 \times 32$ boxes. Another keeps cutting regions in half until they contain sufficiently few objects or until a subdivision limit is reached. Most schemes in use today are **adaptive**, meaning they subdivide more finely in areas that require more detail. Fancy schemes may end up with fewer objects in each region, but they may be slower because figuring out which regions a ray passes through is harder.

The details of any of these techniques aren't important. But because I want you to have a good feel for what space subdivision ray tracing is all about, I'll show you some examples. These examples will use adaptive octree space subdivision. (Each region is a box, and if it's deemed too complex, it's broken into eight little boxes. For a deeper discussion of octrees, refer to page 73.) Adaptive octree space subdivision is a good general-purpose choice because it does well on a wide range of scenes without requiring any user tweaks.

Figure 7.14 is the ray-traced rendering of a simple, contrived scene. Figure 7.15 shows two views of the octree that was built as the scene was rendered. Note how voxels

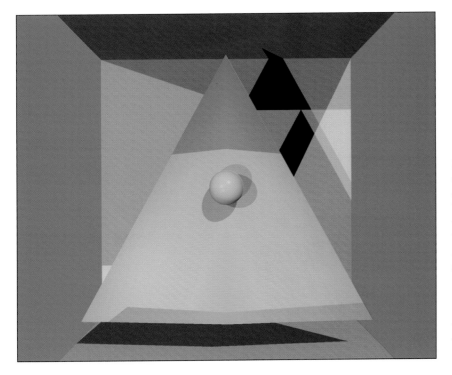

FIGURE 7.14 Ray-tracing a simple, contrived scene.
This is a contrived scene that contains only the "bent triangle" in the middle with a sphere stuck to it, a floor, a back wall, and a ceiling. From the shadows the sphere casts on the triangle, you can see there are three light sources.

(volume elements of an octree, page 73) were subdivided based on the ray activity within the voxel, particularly on the back wall behind the main object where no rays passed by. This shows the adaptive nature of this particular space subdivision algorithm.

Figure 7.16 shows the octree that was built as the scene in Figure 7.12 was rendered.

Radiosity

Radiosity, like ray tracing, tries to keep track of the light bouncing around a scene. The difference is in the kind of light it's suited to handle well.

Because ray tracing follows thin shafts of light (the rays), it deals well with light coming from point sources.

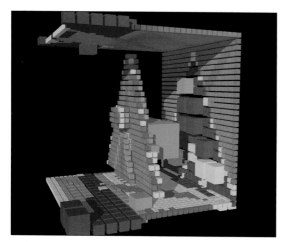
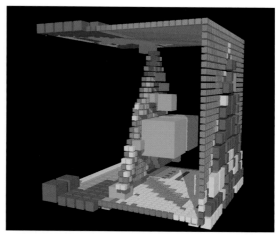

FIGURE 7.15 Resulting octree data structure.

These are two views of the octree data structure that resulted from rendering Figure 7.14. No rays passed through blue voxels since they were created. Yellow means rays did pass through the voxel but didn't hit anything. A blend of red to green indicates the portion of rays that did hit something in that voxel. Red means few hits, with green indicating most hits.

The important thing to note is how the algorithm was adaptive, meaning it didn't waste much time in areas we didn't care about. Look at the part of the back wall that was hidden from view. The voxels there were not subdivided as finely as in places where many rays passed. You can also see this in other areas, such as the back side of the triangular object and the lower-right corner of the floor that was out of the picture.

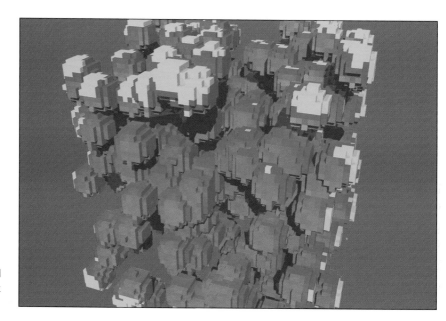

FIGURE 7.16 Octree data structure.

This is the octree data structure that resulted from rendering Figure 7.12. The eye point of the original image would be below and to the left of this picture.

Shadows have sharp edges because the test ray to the light source either gets there or it doesn't. Look around the room, however, and you'll see lots of soft shadows. You should also be able to find some areas that are not directly illuminated by a light source, but aren't completely dark either. The floor under a desk is often like that. It is illuminated by secondary light from the wall or the desk chair, but not directly by a lightbulb or the sun. Radiosity excels at modeling this kind of illumination, called **diffuse reflection** or **secondary scatter**.

In **radiosity rendering**, as in Z-buffer rendering, the scene is decomposed into a pile of polygons. In fact, these polygons will ultimately be rendered using a Z buffer. The difference is in how the object colors are determined.

The radiosity algorithm first computes what portion of the light from each polygon reaches each of the others. In other words, if one polygon were to light up brightly, the algorithm computes how much of that light would directly hit each of the other polygons. This "coupling factor" is determined between every two polygons in the scene. The official term for these coupling factors is **form factors**.

Once the form factors are found, the final visible colors of each of the polygons is determined. This is done by first setting the illumination onto each polygon to 0 (black). The only polygons that wouldn't appear black now are the ones used to model the light sources.

There are lots of variations on how the next step is performed, but basically, the light from the bright polygons causes other polygons to be lit. These, in turn, shine on other polygons, which then shine on more polygons. The form factors are used to determine how much each bright polygon lights up the others. This process of lighting up polygons continues until things settle down. If the process is carried far enough, all the light bouncing around the scene is taken into account. The light reaching the floor under the desk may be coming from the wall, whose light is coming from the ceiling, whose light is coming from a lamp.

There are quite a few variations of the basic algorithm, but these are beyond the scope of this book. What you should remember from this section is the general concept behind radiosity.

Once the final apparent color values for the polygons have been determined, the polygons still need to be drawn. This is usually done with a Z-buffer renderer. Radiosity is therefore really more of a color preprocessing step than it is a rendering method. I've included it in the rendering section because people talk of "radiosity rendering."

You need to look at some pictures to get a better feel for what radiosity can do. Figure 7.17 is a simple scene so that you can better see how the algorithm works. Figures 7.18 through 7.20 are much more complex "real" scenes. In all the images, note the soft shadows. Compare these examples to the ray-tracing example pictures.

WHAT COLOR IS THE OBJECT AT THIS PIXEL?

So far I've mentioned getting an object's color at a particular point, but not how that's actually done. In the next section, "Direct Evaluation (Figuring It Out the Hard Way)," we'll get into those details.

However, directly evaluating the apparent color of an object at a particular point can be an expensive operation. In the section "Interpolation (Fudging It for Most of the Pixels)" on page 122, we'll talk about how to do the expensive evaluation at just a few points, then fill in in-between pixels with reasonable guesses.

 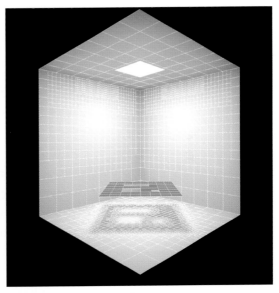

FIGURE 7.17 Radiosity example.
The image on the left shows a simple radiosity scene. Note the soft shadows and that the area in shadow still receives some illumination. The image on the right shows the polygons used in the radiosity calculation. In this particular variant of the radiosity algorithm, polygons are sometimes subdivided if the illumination across them varies too much. This is particularly evident on the floor at the shadow edges.
Image by Kim Wagner Jensen. © 1992, Hewlett-Packard Company.

The process of eventually coming up with pixel color values (as opposed to figuring out which pixels are being drawn) is often called **shading**. By the time we get this deep into the renderer we are always (except for some very rare specialty systems) using the RGB color space (page 3) because it's more convenient mathematically. Color values that were originally specified in another color space have been converted to RGB by now.

Direct Evaluation (Figuring It Out the Hard Way)

In this section we'll talk about how the color of an object is determined at a particular point when viewed from a

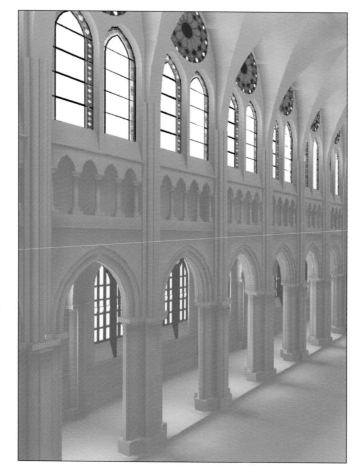

FIGURE 7.18 Radiosity example—Chartres cathedral.
This image is a synthetic reproduction of the Chartres (pronounced "shart") cathedral in Chartres, France.
Image by John Wallace and John Lin. © 1988, Hewlett-Packard Company.

particular direction. The exact physics for this can get pretty hairy, especially if you want to be fairly accurate. Fortunately, in computer graphics we can get quite convincing and useful results without needing to be too accurate. While there are lots of ways to cut a few corners and still get useful results, one method in particular dominates all the others in computer graphics. This method is the Phong lighting model.

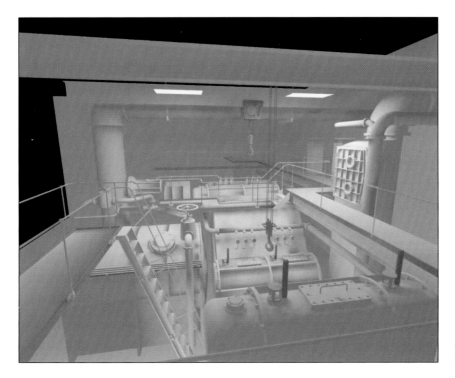

FIGURE 7.19 Radiosity example—Boiler room.
Image by John Wallace, John Lin, and Eric Haines.
© 1990, Hewlett-Packard Company.

The Phong Lighting Model　The **Phong lighting model** is a recipe for computing the apparent color of an object at a particular point. It's important to remember that it's not a description of how the physics works, just a method that produces workable results.

Figure 7.21 is a diagram of the geometric information needed by the Phong lighting model. Note that we can solve only for the apparent color of an object at a particular point. The curvature of the surface therefore doesn't matter, only which way the surface is facing at the point of interest.

Figure 7.21 shows that to find the color at a point, among other things, we need to know which way the surface is facing (**N** vector), where the light is coming from (**L**

FIGURE 7.20 Radiosity example—Printing presses.

Image by John Wallace, Paul Boudreau, and Keith Howei. © 1991, Hewlett-Packard Company.

vector), and where we are looking from (**E** vector). From **N** and **L** we can also compute the reflection vector, which is a handy intermediate result we'll use later. If there is more than one light source in a scene, then we will have one **L** and **R** vector for each light source.

So far all I've said about **N** is that it's the unit surface normal vector. This is true, but which surface are we talking about? If the object's surface is curved, is it the true object surface we are trying to approximate with polygons, for example, or the actual surface made of the polygonal facets?

The answer is that it may be either, although the effects on the final image can be quite different. To avoid confusion, the normal vector used for the purpose of computing the apparent color is called the **shading normal**, and the normal vector of the polygons we are drawing is called the **geometric**

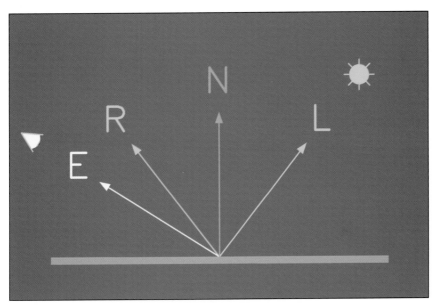

FIGURE 7.21 Phong lighting model geometry.
This diagram shows the geometric information needed by the Phong lighting model to solve for the apparent color at a point. All the vectors shown here are unit vectors, a commonality that simplifies subsequent calculations. (For a refresher on vectors, see page 40). The vector **N** is the surface normal vector. That means it points straight out from the surface. **E** is the eye vector. It points in the direction the point is being viewed from. **L** is the light vector. It points toward the light source. **R** is the reflection vector and points in the direction the light would bounce if the surface were a perfect mirror. **R** is derived from **L** and **N**. (If you know where the light is coming from and which way a mirror is facing, you can figure out which way the light will bounce off the mirror.)

normal. In Figure 7.22, the geometric normal was also used as the shading normal. This strategy is sometimes called **facet shading** because the individual polygons, or facets, become visible. In Figure 7.23, the original surface's normal vectors were used as the shading normals. This strategy is called **smooth shading**. (We can use primitives other than polygons, such as curved patches, to approximate an arbitrary surface. I've been saying polygons just for simplicity.)

Note that the shading normal defines the *apparent* surface orientation in the final image. Our visual systems are finely

FIGURE 7.22 Facet shading example.
In this example, the shading normals are the normals of the surface as it was actually drawn. Note that because each patch in this example is planar, one shading normal applies to an entire patch. The resulting image on the right shows how the as-drawn geometry is very evident with this method.

Note that using the same shading normal for a whole patch doesn't necessarily mean we end up with the same color values for the patch, only the same apparent surface orientation. The color value might change across a patch because the distance to a light source with falloff (page 85) changes, the direction to a light source changes, or the object's apparent color is sensitive to the view angle (specular reflection, which we'll get into later in this section).

tuned to interpret surface shape from subtle shading cues. These shading cues are computed from the shading normal vector, so it controls the surface we think we see, even if that's not really the surface that was drawn geometrically.

The remaining parameters for the Phong lighting model are defined in the object model. These are sometimes called the object **visual properties** or **surface properties**. These are the emissive color, the diffuse color, and the specular color and exponent. I'll describe each of these briefly, then show you some pictures and diagrams with them in action.

The **emissive color** is the color the object appears in the dark, as if it were emitting light. The apparent emissive color is simply the emissive color from the object model. It is not a function of the incoming light, eye direction, or direction the

 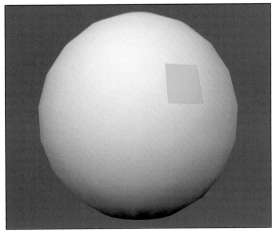

FIGURE 7.23 Smooth shading example.
In this example, the shading normals are the normals of the surface we were trying to model with polygons (a sphere in this case). As part of the modeling step, separate shading normals were specified for each vertex. The shading normal for each vertex is used by all four polygons that share the same vertex. This causes the same apparent color to be computed for each of the four polygons at that vertex. The vertex color values are smoothly blended in the interior of each polygon (we'll get into how this is done on page 125). The image on the right shows how the result can look much closer to the intended surface than what is actually being drawn. Note how the edge of the sphere still shows the individual polygons. This occurs because the silhouette edge is dependent only on the as-drawn geometry, not the shading normal vectors.

surface is facing. Emissive color is used mostly in unusual circumstances.

The **diffuse color** is what you would think of as the "normal" color of an object. As light hits a spot on an object, the diffuse color is reflected equally in all directions. The apparent diffuse color therefore doesn't depend on which direction you are looking from (**E** vector). The direction to the light source, however, does matter. If the light is shining flat onto the surface, it illuminates more than if it is grazing the surface. To be more precise, the effect of the light source is attenuated by the dot product of the **N** and **L** unit vectors. (For a refresher on the dot product, see "Vector Operation: Similarity of Direction," on page 44). Note that when the dot product of **N** and **L** is less than 0, it means the light source is below the surface. That implies the light is occluded by the object, and it is ignored. Visually, the diffuse color is the not-shiny, or matte, color. Cotton cloth is a good example of a substance that exhibits almost pure diffuse reflection.

The **specular color** of an object is reflected mostly around the reflection vector (**R** vector). This loosely models surfaces that show shiny highlights, such as a waxed floor, a car, or some tabletops. A separate parameter, the **specular exponent**, controls how tightly the specular reflection is bunched around the reflection vector, with higher values creating a tighter bunch. A value of 0 causes no bunching at all. Note that this is the same as diffuse reflection because it's reflected equally in all directions. At the other extreme, an infinite specular exponent models pure mirror reflection because everything is reflected exactly along the reflection vector.

The apparent specular color of an object depends on where you're looking from. If you happen to be looking from where the reflection vector is pointing, then you will see the specular color component. As the eye direction (**E** vector) moves off the reflection direction (**R** vector), the contribution from the specular color will fall off. How rapidly it falls off is controlled by the specular exponent. To be more precise, the specular color contribution is proportional to the dot product of the **E** and **R** vectors raised to the power of the specular exponent. The dot product of the **E** and **R** vectors produces a number from 0 to 1, indicating how closely the two vectors are pointing in the same direction. (Actually, the dot product results in a number from −1 to 1, but at values below 0, meaning an angle greater than 90°, the specular contribution is defined to be 0, in which case we abort the specular calculation.) Raising a value between 0 and 1 to a large power will tend to squish it toward 0, while the values exactly at 0 and 1 will remain the same. This effect can be seen in Figure 7.24.

So, what does all this actually look like? In Figures 7.25 through 7.30 you can see examples of surface properties with different combinations of emissive, diffuse, and specular surface properties.

In the remaining examples, each surface property is illustrated by a diagram on the left and the surface property applied to a sphere on the right. In the diagrams, the incoming light is shown as a white arrow. The reflected light is shown as either a yellow arrow or a yellow surface. The surface indicates how much light is reflected in each possible

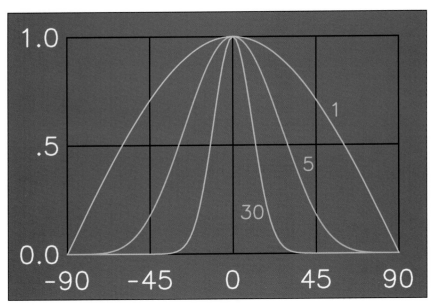

FIGURE 7.24 Plot of specular exponent effect.
These plots show how the specular exponent affects the tightness of the specular highlights. The horizontal axis is the angle between the **E** and **R** vectors in degrees. The three curves were plotted with three different specular exponents, as labeled. The higher the exponent, the more the curve becomes a blip around 0°. This means the eye must be more closely aligned with the reflection direction to see the specular highlight. Note that an exponent of 1 has no effect, so the curve labeled 1 shows the raw dot product of **E** and **R**.

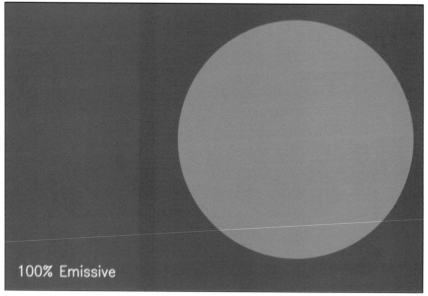

100% Emissive

FIGURE 7.25 Emissive surface property only.
The emissive property doesn't depend on incoming light or view angle. The sphere therefore looks like a disc because each point on the surface is emitting light equally in all directions.

The emissive surface property is not used often, because you rarely want to make it appear that objects are emitting light. I used it in Figure 7.10 to model the lights. I wanted the lights to look bright whether they were in a shadow or not. Note that the emissive surface property can make an object look as if it's emitting light, but, depending on the rendering method, this is different from acting as a light source that can illuminate other objects. Of the rendering methods discussed in this book, only with radiosity would an emissive object also automatically act as a light source.

direction. The more light is reflected in a direction, the farther the surface is in that direction from the center point.

Interpolation (Fudging It for Most of the Pixels)

In the previous section we talked about how to find the apparent color of an object at a particular point. This can be an expensive operation. For diffuse reflection, we have to find the unit surface normal vector and the unit light vector for

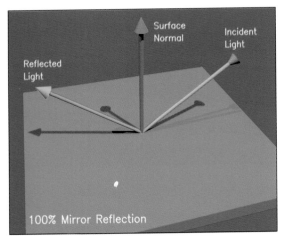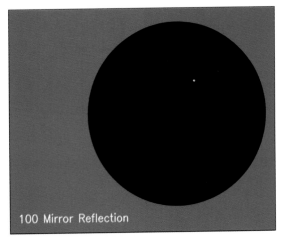

FIGURE 7.26 Pure mirror reflection.
True mirror reflection can't be achieved with the emissive, diffuse, and specular surface properties. I included it here as a counterexample to help you better understand the remaining diagrams. In this case, the incident light is all reflected exactly along the reflection vector.

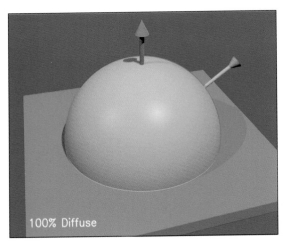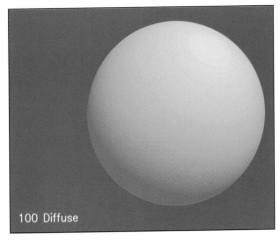

FIGURE 7.27 Pure diffuse reflection.
In diffuse reflection, the incoming light is reflected equally in all directions. The reflected light is therefore no longer shown as an arrow, but as a surface. The yellow surface on the left is exactly a half sphere, indicating the amount of light reflected in each direction is the same.

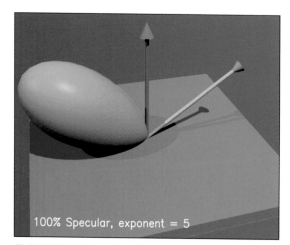

FIGURE 7.28 Specular reflection, exponent = 5.
The specular surface property causes the reflected light to be bunched around the mirror-reflection direction. The tightness of the bunching is controlled by the specular exponent, with higher values causing tighter bunching.

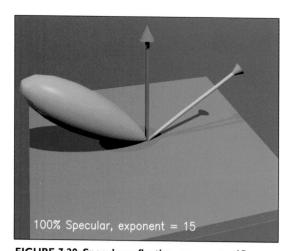

FIGURE 7.29 Specular reflection, exponent = 15.
This is the same surface property as in the previous example, except that the specular exponent was increased from 5 to 15. Note how the reflected light is more tightly bunched around the reflection direction in the diagram at left and how the highlight is smaller on the sphere at right.

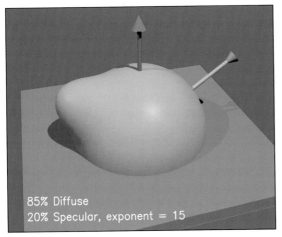
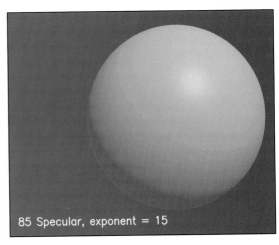

FIGURE 7.30 Mixed diffuse and specular.
The diffuse and specular surface properties are most often used together. Note that they don't have to add to 100 percent. You can usually get away with 105 percent, or even 110 percent, because the brightest part of the specular and diffuse reflections doesn't usually occur on the same spot of the object. In this example, the diffuse color is yellow and the specular color is white. Note how the highlight on the sphere at right looks whiter than the rest of the sphere.

each light source. For specular reflections, we also have to find the unit eye vector and the unit reflection vector, in addition to performing an exponential calculation.

In object-driven rendering methods like Z buffering, we can usually avoid doing this expensive operation for every pixel. We typically compute the real object color only at the vertices of each polygon, then fill in the interior pixels based on the color at the vertices. Strictly speaking, this process should be called **interpolation**—that's the math term for some intelligent process that finds in-between values. However, the different strategies are often referred to as shading. (In computer graphics, the term *shading* is often applied to anything that has to do with making final color values, as opposed to figuring out which pixels to color.)

Flat Shading   **Flat shading** is very simple. The color values from the polygon vertices are averaged, and all the polygon's pixels are set to this fixed (flat) color value. One advantage of flat shading is that it doesn't require the color value to change as the polygon is drawn into the bitmap. This allows the use of polygon-drawing hardware even on low-end 2D display controllers, which can draw each primitive in only one fixed color.

All this simplicity comes at a price, however. The individual polygons are quite visible in the resulting picture, as you can see in Figure 7.31.

Note that there is a difference between flat shading and facet shading (Figure 7.22). In flat shading, each pixel is exactly the same color throughout the polygon. In facet shading, the shading normal vectors used to derive the colors at the vertices are the same, but this may not result in identical vertex colors when the specular surface property is

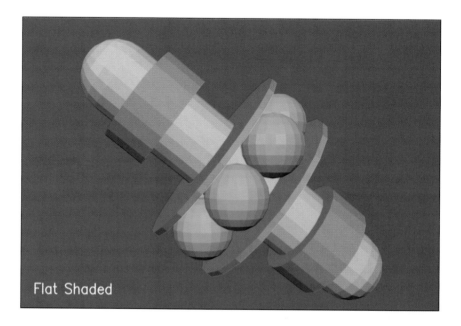

Flat Shaded

FIGURE 7.31 Flat-shading example.

used or when there are point lights or lights with brightness falloff in the scene.

Linear (Gouraud) Shading   In flat shading the color value is held constant for all the pixels in the polygon. In **linear shading**, the rate of change of the color value is held constant for all the pixels in the polygon. This means the color value is increased or decreased the same amount every time you step the same distance and direction in the polygon pixels. For example, red may increase by 5 wherever you move one pixel to the right, or green may decrease by 2 wherever you move one pixel down.

Linear shading is also sometimes called **Gouraud shading,** after Henri Gouraud, who first described a method that included this type of shading in his doctoral thesis. *Linear* is a math term that means the rate of change is held constant. You may also hear this referred to as **linear interpolation** or **bi-linear interpolation,** especially when referring to the low-level pixel issues. The *bi* part of bilinear indicates that linear interpolation is being done in two dimensions.

Figure 7.32 shows a numerical example of bilinearly interpolating a value over a triangle, and Figure 7.33 shows the whole thing in action.

Linear shading is the most common shading technique used with Z-buffer rendering. To support linear shading, $2\frac{1}{2}$D and 3D display controllers (these are defined on page 30) can bilinearly interpolate color values across a primitive in hardware.

Phong Shading   This section is about another shading method: Phong shading. Don't confuse this with the Phong lighting model (page 115). The two are independent, but they happen to be named after the same person.

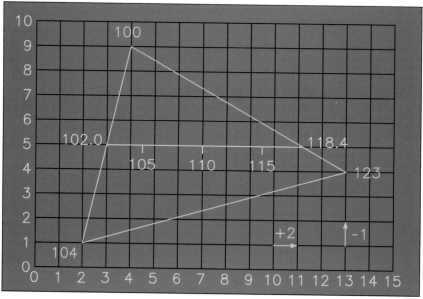

FIGURE 7.32 Bilinear interpolation example.
This is an example of how a value is bilinearly interpolated over a triangle. The values at the vertices are 100, 104, and 123, as shown. One way to think of bilinear interpolation is shown with the white line across the middle of the triangle. First the values at the endpoints of the line (102.0 and 118.4) are found by linearly interpolating the two triangle edges. Then these values are linearly interpolated to yield values in the interior of the triangle.

Another way of thinking about bilinear interpolation is that the value is changed by a fixed amount each time you move one unit in X or one unit in Y. This is shown by the arrows in the lower-right corner. In this example, the value is increased by 2 as you step one unit to the right, and decreased by 1 as you step one unit up.

In **Phong shading,** instead of interpolating the color value for each pixel in a primitive, the shading normal vector is interpolated. Then a separate apparent color computation is performed for each pixel.

This type of shading is relatively rare due to its complexity. Performing an apparent color computation per pixel is well beyond the capability of today's cost-effective hardware. Phong shading was used in some early systems before it was feasible (affordable) to build Z-buffer hardware. It provides better quality results than bilinear interpolation

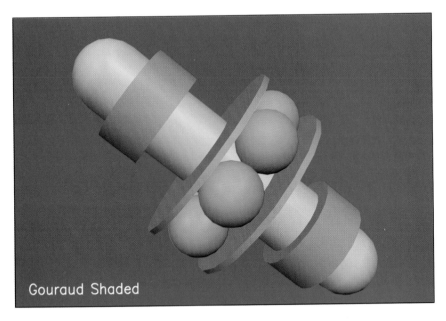

Gouraud Shaded

FIGURE 7.33 Linear-(Gouraud-) shaded example.
Compare this to the flat-shaded example in Figure 7.31. Note how the individual polygons in the model are much less obvious.

with the same primitives. Today, we usually increase shading quality by increasing the tessellation level or by using other rendering methods such as ray tracing. Some high-end 3D rendering packages offer Phong shading as an alternative. While this can enhance the results with the same model, it is significantly slower for two reasons. First, the algorithm itself is complex. Secondly, no mainstream system has hardware support for Phong shading.

Note that ray tracers produce the same object colors as Phong shading does. The shading normal vector is interpolated to whatever location a ray hits on a primitive. This results in the same shading normal vector as if it had been interpolated per pixel in a Z-buffer system. Figure 7.34 was ray-traced to show what Phong shading looks like.

MACH BANDS

Take a look at Figure 7.35. Can you see the white outline in the center of the left triangle? It might help to hold the book

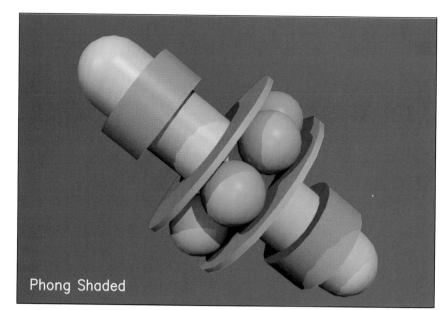

FIGURE 7.34 Phong-shaded example.
This image was ray-traced, which results in the same color values as Phong shading. Try to ignore the shadows in this image, and compare it to Figure 7.33.

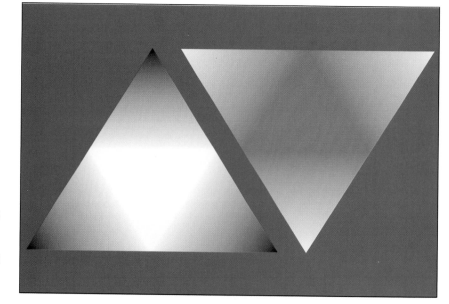

FIGURE 7.35 Mach bands example.
Note the bright line outlining the central region of the left triangle and the dark line outlining the central region of the right triangle. They may be easier to see if you hold the book at arm's length.

at arm's length. Despite what your eyes are telling you, the center of the left triangle is the brightest part and it is *not* outlined in a brighter white. You may be able to see a similar but more subtle effect in the right triangle. The center region of the right triangle is not outlined with a darker color.

The optical illusions you've just seen are called **Mach bands**, named after Ernst Mach, who first reported this effect in 1865. We see Mach bands whenever there is a sudden change in the color's rate of change.

Mach bands can be a particular problem in computer graphics. Remember that in linear shading (page 127) each polygon is drawn with a constant rate of change in the color. Where two polygons meet that have a different rate of color change, there is a sudden jump in the rate of change of the color. This sudden jump causes a Mach band.

Figure 7.36 shows a coarse sphere. Note how each polygon appears to be outlined by bright lines.

Mach bands can be a real pain because there's no easy way to get rid of them. You can use a different shading method, but it's likely more complex, and it's probably not supported in hardware. The common solution is to use more and smaller polygons in modeling. This decreases the difference in the rate of color change between abutting polygons, thus decreasing the Mach bands. This was done in Figure 7.37, but at the cost of about four times more polygons.

COMPOSITING

Sometimes different images need to be **composited**, or blended, into one image. Perhaps the different images were rendered using different techniques, or perhaps they came

FIGURE 7.36 Mach bands example.
This sphere has a bad case of Mach bands. These are the bright lines that appear to outline most of the polygons used to model the sphere. Note that these bright lines are an optical illusion and don't really exist. The model was created using 18 line segments to approximate a circle.

FIGURE 7.37 Decreased Mach bands.
Compare this sphere to the one in Figure 7.36. Mach bands were greatly reduced here by using about four times more polygons. In this image, 36 line segments were used to approximate a circle, whereas only 18 were used in Figure 7.36.

from different sources. Compositing is frequently done in moviemaking and television production. We'll talk about three methods for doing this.

Overlay Where Not Zero

This is the bargain-basement compositing method. Image B is simply written over image A wherever image B doesn't have all 0 pixel values. This method may be adequate for superimposing a title over an existing picture, for example.

This technique is a bit too simplistic for widespread utility. I mention it here only because some inexpensive hardware has this capability built in.

Alpha Buffering

In **alpha buffering**, an additional value is kept per pixel, beyond the color value (and the Z value if you're using Z buffering, described on page 96). This additional value is a fraction that indicates how opaque the pixel is. This is often called the **alpha value**, or sometimes the **transparency value**. I prefer to call it an opacity fraction rather than a transparency fraction because it's almost universally expressed so that 0 means fully transparent (invisible) and the maximum value means fully opaque. This alpha value is commonly stored in 8 bits, which allows for 256 different opacity values (0 to 255). The alpha values for all the pixels in an image or bitmap are called the **alpha buffer**.

Probably the most common alpha-buffering operation is to overlay a new image onto an existing one. How this works at the pixel level is diagrammed in Figure 7.38, and an example is shown in Figure 7.39.

Note that in the alpha overlay example as diagrammed in Figure 7.38, only the overlay image need have alpha values.

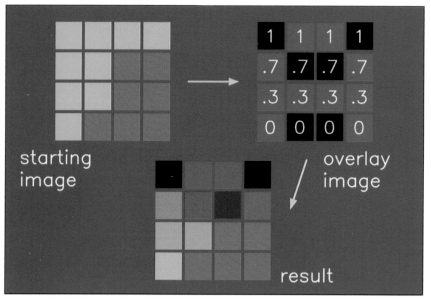

FIGURE 7.38 Alpha overlay diagram.
This diagram shows an alpha-buffer overlay operation. The top right image is overlaid onto the top left one. The number in each pixel of the overlay image indicates the opacity fraction, where 0 means fully transparent (invisible), and 1 means fully opaque. Look at the resulting image and try to understand where each of the colors came from. Note how the top row comes solely from the overlay image (because the overlay is opaque there), and how the bottom row comes solely from the starting image (because the overlay is invisible there).

The starting and resulting images are assumed to be fully opaque. There are a number of other alpha-buffering operations, most of which require all three images to have alpha values. These operations aren't used as often as overlay, and they are beyond the scope of this book.

Alpha-Buffered Rendering   Alpha buffering can also be used during rendering. Instead of a new image composited onto an existing one, you have a new primitive composited onto the existing bitmap. To make this possible, the object's opacity must be described in the modeling step. This way the

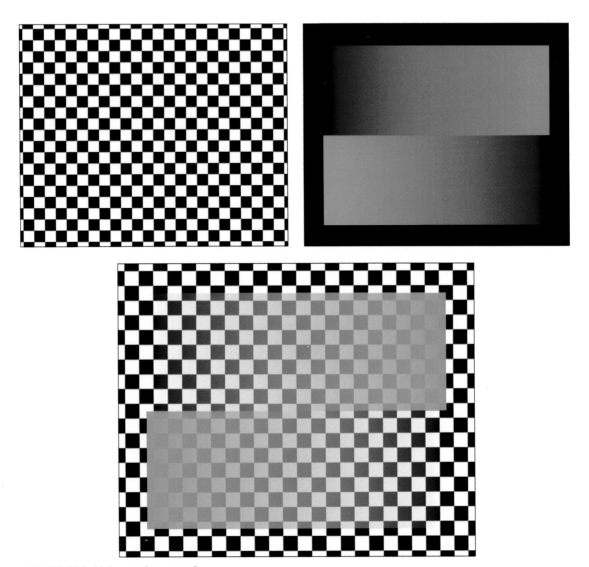

FIGURE 7.39 Alpha overlay example.
This is an example of the same operation as diagrammed in Figure 7.38. The top right image, which contained the two variable-opacity rectangles, was overlaid onto the top left image to yield the bottom image.

renderer can determine the appropriate alpha value for each pixel of each primitive. Figure 7.40 shows an example where some of the primitives are drawn as semitransparent using alpha-buffered rendering.

Chroma Keying

Chroma keying is an image-compositing method used by the television industry before studios had computers or digital video-processing systems. It's therefore not really a computer graphics technique. I've included it here because I want you to realize that image compositing has been around a long time. And, today, most video processing systems are digital, at least on the inside.

In **chroma keying**, the resulting image is taken from the overlay (as opposed to the starting image) whenever the overlay isn't a particular hue (for a reminder of what hue is, see page 4). Another way of saying this is that the starting

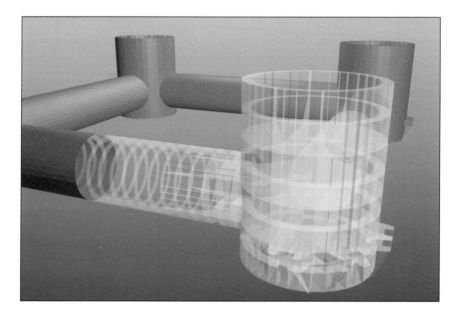

FIGURE 7.40 Alpha-buffered rendering example.

image is shown only where the overlay image is a particular hue.

In the old analog systems, the original and overlay images were really video streams that were fed simultaneously into a box. The box would create the composited output video stream by selecting between the two input streams, depending on the hue of the overlay stream. The way analog video is encoded, it's not too hard to detect a particular hue with analog hardware.

So what do you do with this strange capability? Have you ever seen a newscast where Joe Anchor seems to be standing in front of a live volcano, an armed disagreement in Beirut, or a food fight in the congressional lunchroom? Joe is really safe and snug back in his studio, standing in front of a blue wall, called a **blue screen**, where he can't be shot at or end up wearing the cherry pie. His image with the blue background is chroma-key overlaid onto the video from the remote site. The remote image is displayed wherever Joe's image is blue, meaning the wall behind Joe. This gives the impression of Joe standing in front of whatever is going on.

Blue was chosen because it's the hue most opposite to skin color (or at least to the skin color of the Caucasians who invented the process). Today, having a reporter appear to be at a remote site when he really isn't is considered deceitful. However, chroma keying is still used heavily in television weather reports. Ever wonder how they project that large map behind the weather reporter? The reporter is actually waving his hands in front of a blue wall, with the image of the weather map replacing the blue by chroma keying. This explains why the reporter never points to precise locations on the map or looks directly at the map. The reporter is actually looking at a monitor to make sure he is pointing to New Jersey and not 200 miles out in the Atlantic.

Look carefully at the next television weather report you watch—notice that the reporter isn't wearing anything blue.

ALIASING (THE JAGGIES)

Ever notice how smooth lines in some digital images are jagged and look more like stair steps? That's called **aliasing**, sometimes referred to as the **jaggies**. You can clearly see this effect in Figure 7.41.

Where the Jaggies Come From

Aliasing occurs because the "steps" in the stair steps are individual pixels, which can have only one color throughout, by definition (page 1).

The term *aliasing* comes from signal processing. To truly understand aliasing, you need to know the mathematical

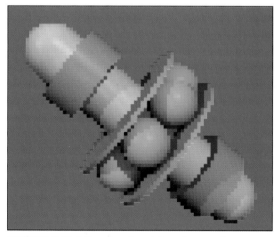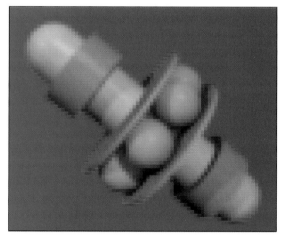

FIGURE 7.41 Aliased and antialiased example.
The left image illustrates aliasing. A technique called *antialiasing* has been applied to the right picture, which makes it a little easier to look at and understand. Both images were deliberately created at very low resolution (80 × 64) so that individual pixels are visible.

foundations of sampling theory and Fourier transforms, and you must learn to think in frequency space. This would take several weeks to cover in a college-level course, and it is way beyond the scope of this book. I'll therefore stick to talking about aliasing in very general, conceptual terms.

How Are Jaggies Avoided?

In this section we'll talk about how to avoid or reduce aliasing, through **antialiasing**. There are several schemes for doing this. In antialiasing, a wide range of trade-offs between computational complexity and resulting quality is possible.

All antialiasing methods do more intelligent things with the pixels than just represent one spot on an object. This can be seen in Figure 7.42.

In the following sections, we'll talk about three representative ways to deal with the jaggies.

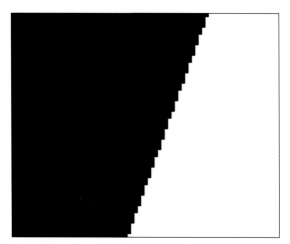 

FIGURE 7.42 Close view of antialiasing.
Both images are of a white polygon on a black background. The polygon edge is completely straight in the model. It's seen as a stair step on the left because whole pixels are set to either the polygon or the background color. The trick in antialiasing is to set pixels near the edge to some intermediate value, as seen in the right image.

Just Ignore Them   I don't mean this to be a flip answer, but ignoring the problem is often a reasonable solution. Are you making an image that many people will see for a long time, or do you just want to look at an answer once? As we'll soon see, antialiasing can require lots of computations and is rarely supported in hardware. Personally, I tend to antialias only "final" pictures. If you've got important detail at the pixel level, you should probably rethink the image anyway.

A Simple Way   All true antialiasing starts with a description of the image at a higher resolution than the final image you're trying to make. One way to do this is to actually render an intermediate image at higher resolution. You now have multiple pixels, called **subpixels**, for each final image pixel. The process of blending several subpixels to make a final pixel is called **filtering** (again, from signal processing).

A simple filtering scheme is to average all the subpixels within a final pixel. This is diagrammed in Figure 7.43.

The filtering method diagrammed in Figure 7.43 is often called a **box filter**. The name comes from the shape of the weighting function.

This method is reasonably fast because an average is relatively simple to compute. The resulting antialiasing quality is medium. Unfortunately, to explain why gets pretty deep into signal processing.

The resulting quality also depends on the number of subpixels per pixel. While you can notice a difference between 2×2 and 3×3 subpixels, there's usually little point in going past 4×4.

A Better Way   As I mentioned, a box filter produces only medium results. Figure 7.44 shows a filter that produces quite good results, although it costs more computationally.

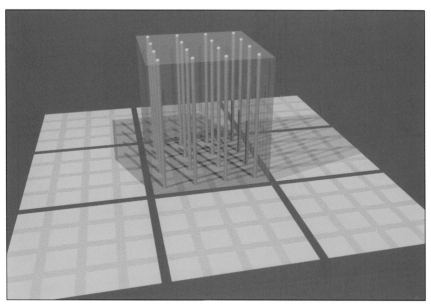

FIGURE 7.43 Box-filtering diagram.
This diagram shows a simple antialiasing filtering scheme. The yellow squares represent the subpixels, with the gray squares underneath the final pixels. The center pixel is computed as the average of all the subpixels within it. The relative weight, or importance, of each subpixel is shown by the vertical bars. In this example, each of the bars is the same height because each subpixel contributes equally to the average. The transparent box shows the continuous weighting function that was applied to the particular subpixels in this example.

This is how most serious antialiasing is done. Note that this kind of antialiasing requires a great deal more computation than just computing an aliased image. First, the renderer must compute more pixels (16 times more at 4×4 subpixels). Then a bunch of subpixels need to be weighted and summed to produce each output pixel.

The math term for this weighted summing operation is **convolution**. The weighting function (the transparent surface in the examples) is usually called the **filter kernel** or the **convolution kernel**.

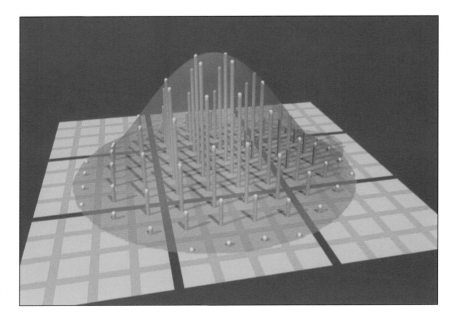

Aliasing in Time

Aliasing is also something that can happen in time if you are doing an animation. Just as each pixel is one fixed color throughout, each frame of an animation is one fixed image throughout. If each frame represents just one instant snapshot in time, then any motion in the animation is really a sequence of frozen steps instead of a smooth motion. This can sometimes be noticeable, and the visual effect has been called *strobing*. The fancy name for aliasing in time is **temporal aliasing**. Wagon wheels that appear to go backward in an old west movie are another visual artifact of temporal aliasing.

The way to reduce temporal aliasing is to have each animation frame represent a small range of time, much as the final pixel in Figure 7.44 ended up representing a small spatial range. Fast-moving objects would then appear blurred, which is the way we tend to perceive them anyway. For example, the spokes in the wagon wheel might appear as one blur, but they would no longer seem to be rotating backward.

Temporal aliasing (and temporal antialiasing) is an advanced topic that's really beyond the scope of this book. I included it just so that you know it exists and to expose you to the term.

TEXTURE MAPPING

Texture mapping is the process of replacing a parameter to the apparent color calculation (page 112) with an external value. The most common form of texture mapping occurs when the object's diffuse color is replaced by an image (the **texture map**), as done in Figure 7.45. The pixels in the texture map are sometimes referred to as **texils** to avoid confusion with the pixels in the image that is being rendered.

Texture mapping requires some additional work in the modeling step. Think about how the renderer knows which part of the texture map belongs on which part of the object. The user defines texture coordinates across the object during modeling. The texture coordinates are interpolated (page 125) across each polygon instead of the final color values. In the case of diffuse color texture mapping, at each pixel, the interpolated texture coordinates are used to identify a specific location in the texture map. The texture map color at this location is used as the object's diffuse color at that pixel.

Note that in this case the texture map color is the object's *diffuse* color, not the final pixel color. The final color depends on the diffuse color and the illumination. For this reason, the total illumination is computed at the vertices of each polygon and also interpolated per pixel. This interpolated illumination is then applied to the color from the texture map to yield the final pixel color. (For more examples, see Figures 7.46 and 7.47.)

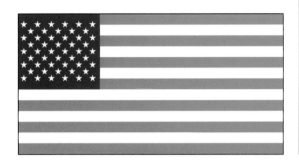

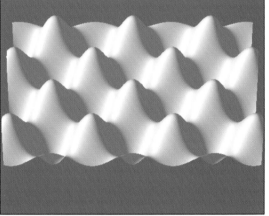

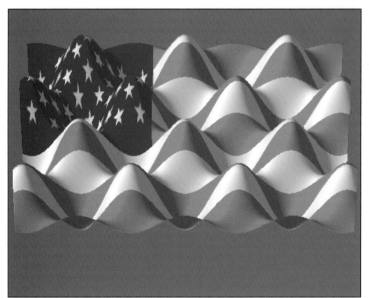

FIGURE 7.45 Diffuse color texture-mapping example.
In this example, the diffuse color of the object at the top right was taken from the texture map at the top left, yielding the image at the bottom.

FIGURE 7.46 Another diffuse color texture-mapping example.
The left image was texture-mapped onto a can to yield the image at right.

Does this sound complicated? It is. But, fortunately, the kinds of operations required per pixel are not too complex. This opens the possibility of reasonably priced hardware implementations. In fact, a few vendors have offered PC graphics cards that do hardware texture mapping for less than $500 in early 1996. By late 1996 the price has dropped, and most vendors have such products.

Other Forms of Texture Mapping

So far, we've talked only about the type of texture mapping where the texture map is an image that replaces the object's diffuse color. This may be the most common and conceptually obvious form, but there are others. Just about any parameter to the apparent color calculation can be texture-mapped.

FIGURE 7.47 Texture-mapping example.
There are a number of texture-mapped objects in this image, including the countertop, bricks, floor, salt, and can of tomatoes. Texture mapping adds significant visual detail to the image without the need for modeling more complex geometry. Note how the countertop, floor, and wall would be flat, featureless planes without texture mapping.
© 1986, Eric Haines and Donald P. Greenburg, Program of Computer Graphics, Cornell University.

Texture-mapping small perturbations of the shading normal vector (page 116) is called **bump mapping**. Because the shading normal vector defines the apparent surface orientation, bump mapping can make an object appear to be rougher than it really is geometrically. This was done in Figures 7.48 and 7.49.

Note that in bump mapping the texture isn't an image because it doesn't contain color values. In other forms of texture mapping, the texture may be a function instead of an explicit table of values (like an image). This is often done when the texture is three-dimensional. A **3D texture** is also

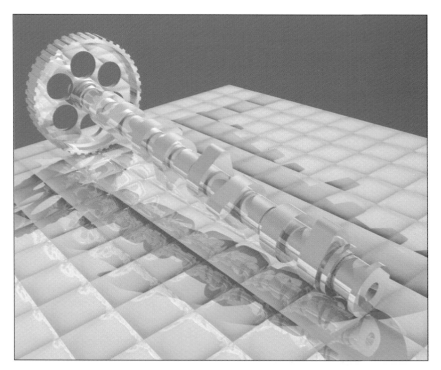

FIGURE 7.48 Bump-mapping example. The surface below the camshaft was bump-mapped. Note how it appears to be tiled with pillow-shaped objects although it is flat geometrically. You can see that it's actually flat by looking closely at the shadows. This occurs because the shadows depend on the true geometry, not on the shading normal vectors. *Rendered by Eric Haines. © 1988, Hewlett-Packard Company.*

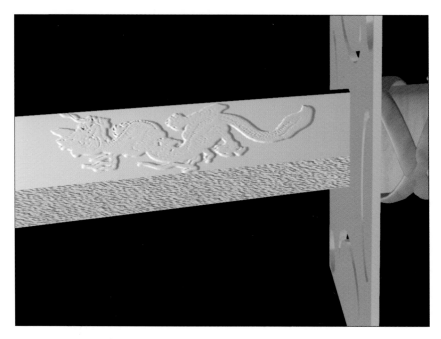

FIGURE 7.49 Bump-mapping example. The dragon on this sword blade was bump-mapped. *Image by Nathaniel Wieselquist, class of 1996, Westford Academy, the public high school in Westford, Massachusetts.*

called a **solid texture**. Such textures have been used to simulate marble and wood grain.

DITHERING

Dithering is a technique for trading off spacial resolution to get more color (or gray-scale) resolution. What if you wanted to display a continuous-tone gray-scale image, but each pixel could be only black or white? You could decide to make a white pixel wherever the gray value was above half and a black pixel wherever it was below half. The image would look very splotchy and even might not be recognizable.

For many applications, dithering provides a better way. Suppose you treated each clump of 2×2 pixels as a unit. You could then set 0, 1, 2, 3, or 4 of the pixels to white and the rest to black. When viewed as an aggregate, each clump now can have five different gray levels.

One way to decide whether a pixel should be black or white is to imagine different threshold values for each pixel in the clump. For example, the lower-left pixel becomes white if the continuous gray value there is .2 or greater, the upper right is .4, upper left is .6, and lower right is .8. These thresholds are called the **dither pattern**. Just such a dither pattern was used in Figure 7.50.

Note that the apparent gray-scale resolution was increased at the expense of adding a pattern, or graininess, to the image. This technique isn't limited to black and white or 2×2 clumps of pixels. It can be used to increase color or gray-scale resolution, regardless of how many levels are available. (See Figure 7.51 for another example.)

FIGURE 7.50 Black-and-white dithering example.
The black-to-white ramp on the left requires many shades of gray for an accurate representation. The image on the right approximates the ramp with five different gray levels, even though each pixel is either black or white. Five gray levels (instead of two) are achieved by using a 2 × 2 dither pattern.

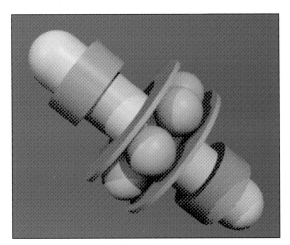 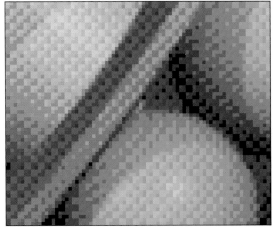

FIGURE 7.51 Color dithering example.
Both these images contain only 240 different colors. A 4 × 4 dither pattern was used to give the appearance of almost continuous color resolution. The graininess noticeable in the left image is a disadvantage of dithering. There's no free lunch. The right image is a magnification of the central region of the left image so that you could better see the dither pattern.

The dither pattern can be a tile of any size, or it doesn't need to be a tile at all. Some dithering methods are based on random patterns. The intricacies of various dithering techniques are beyond the scope of this book. However, it's worth remembering what dithering is and the general flavor of how it's done.

8

Animation

Images are animated by showing many of them in rapid succession. This gives the illusion of a moving image. In North America, Japan, and other countries that use the NTSC video standard, 30 new images are shown every second on television. (Due to interlacing we are actually shown a new half-image every $1/60$ second. See page 17 for a discussion of interlacing.) Most other countries use the PAL or SECAM video standards that show 25 frames per second. Movies use 24 different images per second. But to decrease the apparent flicker, each image is shown twice so that the screen flashes 48 times per second.

Even though animations are composed of individual still images, there are unique issues to animation beyond making lots and lots of images. That's what this chapter is about.

Most of the special considerations for animation occur in modeling. Sometimes a clever renderer gets involved for efficiency, but that's beyond the scope of this book. The basic problem is how to describe and control the motion of objects and other scene elements. There are many methods for achieving this. We'll talk about three that you might bump into.

KEY FRAMES (WYSIWYG METHOD)

In **key-frame animation systems**, the positions and other parameters of scene elements are exactly defined for certain **key frames**. The parameters are then interpolated to obtain values for the in-between frames.

For example, if you were making an animated cartoon where a character is raising an arm, you might specify the shoulder angle to be 0° at frame 100 and 90° at frame 250. This means that frames 100 and 250 are key frames and that the shoulder angle will be interpolated from 0 to 90° between frames 100 and 250. If other objects or scene elements (the light sources, camera point, etc.) are to move during this time, they too would have to be defined at frames 100 and 250.

An important consideration in key-frame animation is how the key-frame parameters are interpolated to obtain the values for the remaining frames. The conceptually obvious approach is to change each parameter by a fixed step each frame. In math terms, this would be called *linear interpolation.* Unfortunately, this produces very jerky motion that seems to suddenly start, stop, and change direction. One better method is called *cubic interpolation.* It avoids sudden starts, stops, or changes in direction. Linear and cubic interpolation are compared in Figure 8.1.

Key-frame systems are relatively intuitive, simple to use, and easy to implement—they are popular for those reasons. You can think of key framing as the WYSIWYG (what you see is what you get) of animation systems.

PARAMETRIC (RULE-BASED METHOD)

Sometimes you may need more accurate control over an animation than key frames can provide. In a key-frame

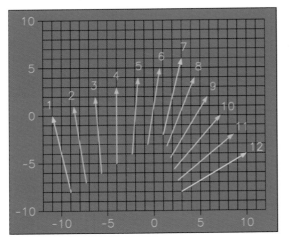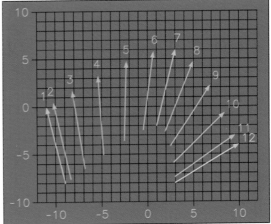

FIGURE 8.1 Linear and cubic frame interpolation.
Linear frame interpolation is shown on the left, and cubic on the right. In both these examples, the motion of the arrow is specified at three key frames: 1, 7, and 12. The arrow is shown yellow at the key frames and gray at the in-between frames. Note the sudden change in direction at frame 7 on the left, and the smoothness of the motion on the right. Note also how the motion slowly starts and stops on the right.

system, the interpolation for the in-between frames may not result in the exact motion you had in mind.

In **parametric animation systems,** you provide rules for how to determine each animated value at any point in time. The animation system then queries the rules at each frame, supplying the time value at that frame. The term *parametric* refers to the fact that the rules are based on input parameters, particularly the animation time value. The rules are usually described by mathematical equations or by computer routines. A computer routine was used in Figure 8.2.

Defining the motion in Figure 8.2 accurately using key frames would have been more difficult with most systems. You would have had to figure out the exact ball position at the key frames yourself. The key frames would also need to be carefully positioned so that the interpolation between frames would be a close approximation to the actual ball position.

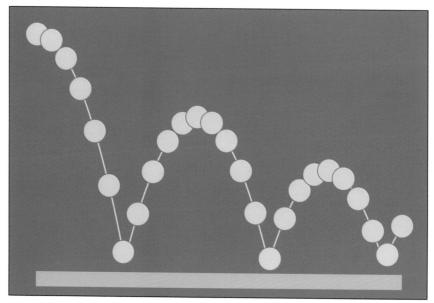

FIGURE 8.2 Parametric animation example.
This example demonstrates a parametric animation of a bouncing ball. A computer routine was written that calculates the ball's position for any specific instant in time. The animation system queried the computer routine once for each of the 26 frames in the animation. The ball's position at each frame is shown with a yellow disc, while the continuous path is shown in gray.

INVERSE KINEMATICS AND DYNAMICS (PHYSICS KNURD METHOD)

In key-frame animation, we figured out the scene state at selected frames, and the computer guessed for the in-between frames. In parametric animation we had to explicitly describe how the scene state changed as a function of animation time. With the **inverse kinematics** or **inverse dynamics methods,** the computer actually calculates some of the motion automatically.

For example, suppose you were making an animation of a robot picking up a block and putting it into a bin. You would first describe how the various linkages in the robot's arm are connected and how they are allowed to move relative to each other. These rules about how the system functions are called **constraints**. You would then describe the motion of the robot's hand, and the computer would figure out how all the linkages have to move so that the hand ends up where you specified.

FIGURE 8.3 Inverse kinematics example.
The top left, top right, and lower-left frames show a simulated human turning a steering wheel. Once all the system constraints were defined, the animator specified how the wheel should turn and that the hand must remain holding the same spot on the wheel. The computer figured out the wrist, elbow, and shoulder angles and positions by inverse kinematics. In the lower-right frame the seat is moved back from the upper-right frame. Again, note how the elbow, shoulder, wrist joint, and right leg were automatically adjusted.
Images by Mike Hollick. © 1996, Center for Human Modeling and Simulation, University of Pennsylvania. Reprinted with permission.

So far I've described inverse kinematics. Inverse dynamics systems not only understand how objects are connected, but they also incorporate things such as friction, and collisions. The term *inverse* means that the computer is figuring out what the objects must have done to achieve an end result you specify. *Forward* dynamics would be defining the properties of the ball and the green surface in Figure 8.2, then letting the ball go with a particular velocity so that the computer could calculate the bounces without your explicitly having to program them.

As an example of inverse dynamics, imagine a chain lying on the floor. The computer is told only that each link is connected to its neighbors and how friction and collisions between the links works. You now specify that the two end links are raised up off the floor. The computer will determine the motion of all the individual links by inverse dynamics. Initially the chain will dangle back and forth, but eventually it will settle down (because of the friction) to a nice curve between the two endpoints. (By the way, the shape of this curve is called a *catenary*.)

Figure 8.3 shows an example of inverse kinematics in action.

9

Saving the Pixels
(Image File Issues)

We've talked about how renderers write into a bitmap, but not how to get the final bitmap out where you can access it. Generally, bitmaps are written to **image files**. Several standard image file formats have evolved that make it easier to store, transmit, and exchange digital images. This chapter talks about some of the issues in saving images to image files.

COMMON IMAGE FILE STRATEGIES

Even though there is a great deal of variation in how data is encoded in different image file formats, some commonalities do exist. We'll talk about them in this section.

Just about all image file formats store the pixels in **scan-line order**. That means all the pixels for one horizontal scan line are written before going on to the next scan line. A **scan line** is just another name for a horizontal row of pixels.

Most file formats (but definitely not all) store pixels in left-to-right order within a scan line, and most store the scan lines in top-to-bottom order.

Most file formats have the option of storing both **palette** or true color images. Palette in this usage means the same thing as pseudo color. (True color and pseudo color are discussed on page 25.) The most common true color format is 8 bits per primary (red, green, blue) per pixel. Such a color is essentially continuous (you can't distinguish individual colors) for everyday applications and is handy because most computers can efficiently handle 8-bit numbers. Some specialized imaging applications require 10 to 12 bits per primary per pixel.

COMPRESSION

Computer graphics is a great way to eat up disk space. A 1,280 × 1,024 true color image with 8 bits per color per pixel contains about 4 megabytes. Now imagine an animation. A true color video frame is about 648 × 486 pixels, which comes to a total of 0.94 megabytes. That doesn't sound too bad until you remember that you need 30 of them every second. That comes out to 28 megabytes per second of animation. A 1-minute animation therefore contains 1.7 gigabytes of data.

Fortunately, there is something we can do about it while we're waiting for a $200 terabyte hard drive. The color value of most pixels is close to the color value of adjacent pixels. In other words, most images have a great deal of redundant information. This makes them good candidates for compression algorithms.

There are many different compression algorithms, but they can all be put into one of two broad categories: lossless and lossy.

Lossless Compression

Lossless compression preserves all image data. This means you can compress and uncompress an image as many times as you want and still end up with the same original pixel values. There are a number of lossless compression algorithms. We'll briefly talk about the two you'll bump into most often.

Runlength **Runlength compression**, also called **runlength encoding**, reduces storage for successive pixels that have exactly the same value. This is done by storing the pixel value only once, but with a repeat count indicating how many pixels in a row should have this value.

Runlength compression works reasonably well on computer-generated images, especially ones that have large areas of background with the same value horizontally. Because pixels are usually stored in horizontal scan lines, this causes adjacent pixels to have the same value, which allows runlength compression to be effective. The image in Figure 9.1 was compressed 7.6 : 1 with runlength compression.

Runlength compression usually doesn't work well on scanned images because they often have slight differences between adjacent pixels.

LZW LZW stands for Lempel-Ziv and Welch, the people who were involved in its development. The general method was described by Terry A. Welch in a paper that appeared in June 1984. LZW compression was long assumed to be in the public domain when a number of image file formats adopted it. Unisys Corporation now claims that LZW is covered by its U.S. patent number 4,558,302 and has recently gotten several large companies to pay royalties for LZW software. It's still not clear how this will affect the industry and LZW compression use.

The details of LZW compression are beyond the scope of this book, but it works by identifying and compressing repeating patterns in the data. For example, if the pattern red-pink-blue-gray appeared often enough, it would eventually be replaced by just one number. The patterns grow each time they are referenced. For example, after the first time red-pink-blue-gray is encountered, red-pink may be identified as a pattern. The second time, the red-pink pattern is referenced by one number and red-pink-blue is identified as a pattern. The next time, red-pink-blue is referenced by one number and red-pink-blue-gray is identified as a pattern. I've grossly oversimplified how LZW works, but that's the basic flavor.

LZW compression works well on a variety of images, including scanned and dithered (page 148) images. Figure 9.1 was compressed 7.8 : 1 with LZW compression. This is only slightly better than runlength compression, because Figure 9.1 is the kind of image with which runlength compression works reasonably well.

Lossy Compression

Lossy compression schemes are called that because they lose some of the data during compression. This allows them to achieve higher compression ratios than lossless schemes.

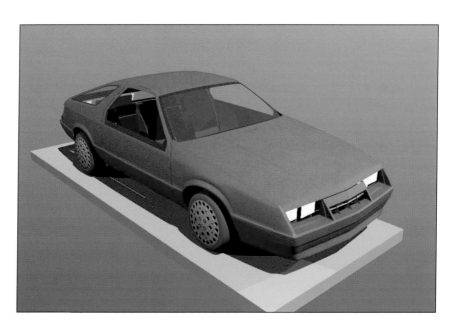

FIGURE 9.1 Lossless compression example. This is a full-color image with 8 bits per color per pixel and contains 1,280 × 853 pixels. Uncompressed, it would require 3,275,520 bytes of storage. A runlength encoded image file reduced this by 7.6 times, and an LZW compressed image file by 7.8 times.

Many lossy compression schemes try to lose data in a way that is least likely to be noticed by the human visual system. A good everyday example of this is color television, although it's not a scheme for digital images. The color information is blurred more (yielding higher compression) than the intensity information because people are not as sensitive to blurred color as they are to blurred intensity.

Most lossy schemes for image file formats also allow a trade-off between compression ratio and image fidelity. The higher the compression ratio, the more compression artifacts become visible in the image.

Lossy compression schemes are by no means limited to the two mentioned here. I picked these two because you're most likely to hear about them as a means for compressing digital color images.

JPEG   JPEG is probably the most common lossy compression scheme for digital color images, although the details of how it works are beyond the scope of this book. (JPEG stands for Joint Photographic Experts Group.)

A nice feature of JPEG is that you can trade off compression ratio with image fidelity. The image in Figure 9.2 was compressed about 77:1 from the raw data. This is a relatively high compression ratio, resulting in fairly obvious compression artifacts. Generally, compression ratios of 10:1 result in images where the compression artifacts can be ignored for most applications.

MPEG   MPEG (an acronym for Motion Picture Experts Group) is similar to JPEG compression, except that it works on motion picture sequences, while JPEG works on individual images. Just as there is redundant information from pixel to pixel, redundant information occurs from frame to

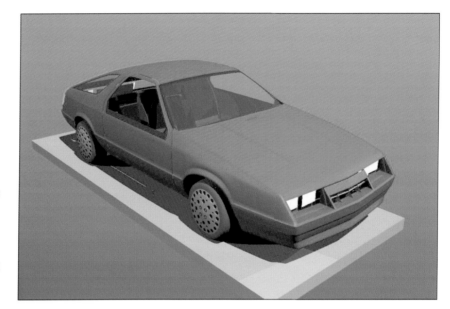

FIGURE 9.2 JPEG compression example. This is the same image as in Figure 9.1, except that this one was compressed 77:1 using the JPEG scheme. This is a fairly high JPEG compression level. Compression artifacts are clearly visible at the bottom of the door and the fender in front of the front wheel.

frame of an animation. MPEG exploits this interframe redundancy to achieve higher compression ratios than JPEG for equivalent image-fidelity loss. Also, humans are more tolerant of some kinds of artifacts in animated images than in still images. This tolerance allows even higher compression ratios than with JPEG for the same apparent quality level.

10

Where to Go from Here

As I said in the beginning, this book is about the technology of computer graphics, not about any particular system or application. I felt it was important to stick to that approach for three main reasons.

First, although there are plenty of how-to books for various systems, I could find no approachable introduction to the basics for the average computer user. I've sometimes taught computer graphics to beginners, and I've never had a good answer to the question, "Can you recommend a good introductory book?"

Second, the basics of the technology are common to every particular use. It makes sense to start here, even if all you're interested in is a particular system. The texts for specific systems rarely give a good background, and when they do, it's usually from their own narrow perspective.

Third, the technology shouldn't become dated so quickly. Just a few years ago, Truevision Targa files were the predominant image file format. Now we're onto TIFF and JPEG, and who knows what next year's "standard" will be. But Z buffers have been Z buffers for at least 15 years, and they will probably still be around mostly unchanged in another 15. It's just not economically feasible to put this kind of effort into a book that only has a three-year life span.

WHAT'S HOT

However, I understand that the technology isn't an end unto itself. In this section, I'll break my own rules and briefly mention some of the buzzwords you might hear that relate to particular systems, applications, or standards. In most cases, I won't give references, because these come and go even faster than what they describe. I find it impossible to keep up with new material as it becomes available. I'd rather not say anything than steer you in the wrong direction.

To find the latest reference on a particular topic, the best strategy is to ask around. Remember, a few months can be a long time in this business. You might start with a knowledgeable staff member at a bookstore that has a large computer section. But this industry is too big for any one person to know more than a few niches in depth. You need to find someone who knows about the particular niche that interests you.

A good way to find such people is at meetings of professional societies. The best one for computer graphics is ACM/SIGGRAPH. ACM is the world's oldest computer society (**SIGGRAPH** stands for Special Interest Group on Graphics). SIGGRAPH has local chapters in some major cities in the United States, and even a few worldwide. Attending a meeting of a SIGGRAPH local chapter is probably the best single way to meet others who can help you learn more about computer graphics. For those of you who are Internet-enabled, you can reach them at http://siggraph.org.

The Internet

There's been an explosion of interest in the **Internet** and the **World Wide Web**, often referred to as *WWW*, or *the*

Web. The Web is a bunch of interconnected documents on the Internet. These documents are written in a formatting language called **HTML**, which stands for HyperText Markup Language. These HTML documents need to be read by special software, called a **Web browser**, which lets you see them on your screen and navigate from one document to another. Some people wanted to see more than the text and images HTML provides, so they came up with a new standard called **VRML**, which stands for Virtual Reality Modeling Language. VRML allows documents to include 3D computer graphics that you can tumble around and "walk through." The next step is something called Java. It's a standard way for describing actions your computer can take with regard to the particular document you are viewing. Java can allow you to interact with the document in complicated ways as programmed by the document author.

Image File Formats

You are likely to bump into two common image file formats that use lossless compression (page 158), TIFF and GIF. **TIFF** stands for Tag Image File Format, and **GIF** stands for Graphics Interchange Format. TIFF is probably the most broadly accepted format for importing images into applications. GIF, which is owned by CompuServe Incorporated of Columbus, Ohio, was originally intended as an efficient means for downloading images via a modem.

The common image file formats that employ lossy compression (page 160) are JPEG for still pictures and MPEG for animation sequences. These were discussed earlier starting on page 161.

Systems

The vast majority of installed computer systems are PCs that run some form of the Microsoft Windows operating systems. Therefore, the most common graphics system is the Windows graphics system. Unix systems almost universally run some form of the X Window system, usually just called **X Windows**. Both Windows and X Windows provide window management and 2D drawing capabilities to applications. The most accepted 3D graphics library is Silicon Graphics' **OpenGL**, sometimes just called GL (GL was actually the name of the proprietary library OpenGL was based on, but that's ancient history at this point). Microsoft is now including a GL interface in its most advanced system, Windows NT.

YOUR TURN

I hope this book has given you a sound foundation, one that will support you well as you learn more. Computer graphics is a big world that is becoming accessible to ever growing numbers of people. The field is continually evolving, with many opportunities for individuals to make contributions. Now it's time to see what *you* can do. Go for it!

Glindex

CROSS-INDEX OF GRAPHICS TERMS

This section is a combined glossary and index. Many of the keywords listed here are set in bold type where they are first defined in the text.

3D texture   146

A texture map that is a function of three variables. This is also called a *solid texture* because the texture map is a volume. Solid textures have been used in diffuse color texture mapping to simulate things such as marble and wood grain. Sometimes, specifying the color in a volume is simpler than specifying it on the surface of an object, especially if the object has a complex shape.

3D transform   48

The act of converting the coordinates of a point, vector, etc., from one coordinate space to another. The term can also refer collectively to the numbers used to describe the mapping of one space on another, which are also called a *3D transformation matrix*.

3D transformation matrix   48

See *3D transform*.

adaptive space subdivision   108

Space subdivision refers to the process of breaking up the scene space into many small regions. Adaptive means this is done only where and when needed, instead of in a fixed way up front. Adaptive space subdivision is often used by ray tracers. Octrees and BSP trees are examples of subdivision algorithms that can be adaptive.

addition, vector   42

See *vector addition*.

aliasing   138

The phenomenon that makes smooth lines and edges appear stair-stepped or jagged. Aliasing is also called the *jaggies*.

aliasing, temporal   142

See *temporal aliasing*.

alpha buffer   133

The collective name for the alpha values for every pixel of an image or bitmap.

alpha-buffered rendering   134

Using an alpha buffer for rendering, as opposed to for image compositing or matting. Alpha-buffered rendering implies the ability to render semitransparent primitives.

alpha buffering   133

The process of rendering or compositing images using an alpha buffer. An alpha buffer supplies an opacity fraction for every pixel.

alpha value 133

The alpha buffer value for a single pixel. An alpha value is a value indicating the pixel's opacity. Zero usually represents totally transparent (invisible), and the maximum value represents completely opaque. Alpha values are commonly represented in 8 bits, in which case transparent to opaque ranges from 0 to 255.

ambient light 88

A light source that shines equally on everything. This is a hack used to give some illumination to areas that are not in direct view of any light source. In the real world, such areas are illuminated indirectly by light bouncing off other objects. Ambient illumination is commonly used, except in radiosity rendering because radiosity actually computes light bouncing between objects.

AND operator 68

A constructive solid geometry (CSG) modeling operation on two objects. The resulting object exists only where both input objects existed. This operation is also called INTERSECTION.

animation 151

Any method that can make an image appear to change over time. In computer graphics, this is done by showing many still images in rapid succession. This produces the illusion of a moving, or animated, image.

animation, inverse dynamics 154

See *inverse dynamics.*

animation, inverse kinematics 154

See *inverse kinematics.*

animation, key-frame 152

See *key-frame animation.*

animation, parametric 153

See *parametric animation.*

antialiasing 139

The process of reducing aliasing, or jaggies, in creating an image.

antialiasing filter, box 140

A box filter used in antialiasing averages all the samples of a high-resolution image within each resulting pixel. All the samples are weighted equally over a rectangular region, usually the resulting antialiased pixel. Box filtering provides fair- to medium-quality results, but it is much less complex than higher-quality methods.

antialiasing filter, good-quality 140

A good-quality antialiasing filter blends values from a high-resolution image such that samples near the resulting pixel center are weighted more than others. Sample weights smoothly approach 0 at a distance of about $1\frac{1}{4}$ pixels.

antialiasing filter, simple 140

See *antialiasing filter, box.*

apparent color determination 112

See *color determination.*

apparent surface orientation 117

The orientation (which direction it's facing) a surface appears to have in an image. This is controlled by the shading normal vector, which is not necessarily the same as the normal vector of the primitive as it's actually drawn (the geometric normal vector).

B-spline 65

A particular type of spline, the mathematical details of which are beyond the scope of this book.

back end 23

See *video back end.*

basis vector 50

A vector that defines one axis of a coordinate system. Three basis vectors, one each for the X, Y, and Z axes, are needed to define a 3D coordinate system. A basis vector indicates the length and direction of a +1 increment in its axis.

beam current 8

The current of an electron beam in a cathode-ray tube. The current is the number of electrons per unit time, which is usually measured in milliamperes. A higher beam current produces a brighter phosphor dot.

beta spline 65

A particular type of spline, the mathematical details of which are beyond the scope of this book.

bicubic patch 64

A particular type of surface patch. Bicubic surface patches can have curved edges, as opposed to polygons, which always have straight edges. The mathematical details of bicubic patches are beyond the scope of this book.

biquadratic patch   64

A particular type of surface patch. Biquadratic surface patches can have curved edges, as opposed to polygons, which always have straight edges. The mathematical details of biquadratic patches are beyond the scope of this book.

bilinear interpolation   127

Interpolation is the process of determining plausible in-between values, given explicit values at particular points. Linear means that the values fall along a line from one known point to the next. This means the value changes a fixed amount for a fixed-sized step. Bilinear means this process is carried out in two dimensions. In computer graphics, bilinear interpolation is often applied to find color values at the interior pixels of a primitive. The apparent color values are computed explicitly at the vertices of a polygon and are bilinearly interpolated in the polygon's interior. Bilinear interpolation of pixel color values is also called *Gouraud shading*.

binary space partition   75

See *BSP tree*.

bitmap   27

The collective name for all the stored pixels in a display controller. The bitmap is also the interface between the display controller's drawing front end and its video back end. The term bitmap is also used in general to refer to any 2D array of pixels.

blobbies   67

A name sometimes applied to potential functions used in modeling objects.

blue screen   137

A background often used for photographs or video that are to be matted, or composited, over other images. A blue background is almost universally used in chroma-keying video compositing.

Boolean operator   68

A mathematical operator that works on true or false values. Boolean operators are also called *logical operators*. In computer graphics, constructive solid geometry (CSG) operators may also be called Boolean operators. Some common CSG operators are AND, OR, NOT, and XOR.

bounding volume 107

A volume that encloses multiple 3D primitives. If the bounding volume doesn't intersect an object of interest (such as a ray in ray tracing), then the objects within the bounding volume are guaranteed to also not intersect the object, eliminating the need to check explicitly.

box filter 140

See *antialiasing filter, box.*

BSP tree 73

A hierarchical method of subdividing a volume. BSP stands for *binary space partition.* In this method, the volume is originally represented as one whole. If more detail is needed, the volume is subdivided into two volumes. Each of these are further subdivided into two volumes if more detail is needed. The process is repeated until the desired level of detail is achieved or an arbitrary subdivision limit is reached.

BSP tree, regular 75

A special form of BSP tree where all the volume elements are rectangular solids that are always subdivided exactly in half along one of their three major axes.

bump mapping 146

A form of texture mapping where the texture supplies small perturbations of the shading normal vector.

calligraphic 95

An early type of computer graphics display that could draw only lines, not filled-in areas. Calligraphic displays are rarely used today and have mostly been replaced by raster displays.

camera point 88

See *eye point.*

cathode-ray tube 7

A type of vacuum tube that is commonly used as a computer graphics output device. A thin beam of electrons is shot at a spot on the inside of the tube's face. The inside of the face is coated with phosphors that emit light when the beam hits them. The beam is swept in a raster pattern to hit every spot on the screen.

The beam current is modulated to make light and dark areas on the phosphors, forming an image. Cathode-ray tube is usually abbreviated as CRT.

chroma keying 136

An image-compositing technique commonly used on video signals. An overlay video signal is selected instead of a background video signal whenever the overlay isn't a particular preset hue, usually blue. Action shot in front of a blue screen can thereby appear on top of the background signal.

color determination 112

The process of figuring out what the apparent color of a particular point on a particular primitive is. This process is used to answer the question "What color is the object at this pixel?"

color, diffuse 119

See *diffuse color.*

color, emissive 118

See *emissive color.*

color, specular 120

See *specular color.*

color index value 25

The input value to a color lookup table (LUT) of a display controller's video back end operating in pseudo color mode. Color index values are also referred to as *pseudo colors.*

color lookup table 25

A table of color values in a display controller's video back end. In pseudo-color mode, it translates the pseudo color values into RGB color values. In true-color mode it becomes three separate tables, one for each red, green, and blue component. It then translates the red, green, and blue pixel component values to the final displayed red, green, and blue component values. The color lookup table is usually just called the LUT.

color purity 12

The degree to which a color CRT can display just one of its three red, green, or blue primary colors without displaying any portion of the other two. This is a measure of how accurately each electron gun can hit only the phosphor dots of its color.

color space   3
> A scheme for describing different shades or colors. The RGB color space defines a shade as a mixture of specific quantities of red, green, and blue.

color space, RGB   3
> See *RGB*.

color space, IHS   4
> See *IHS*.

color wheel   5
> A circular diagram of colors. The hue varies as the angle within the disc. Saturation increases from the center outward. The entire disc is usually shown at the same intensity.

compositing   131
> The process of combining two images to yield a resulting, or composite, image. Alpha buffering is a common compositing technique in computer graphics.

compression   158
> As used in this book, the process of encoding an image that contains redundant information such that it requires less storage. Runlength and LZW encoding are examples of lossless compression techniques. JPEG and MPEG are examples of lossy compression techniques.

compression, JPEG   161
> See *JPEG*.

compression, lossless   158
> See *lossless compression*.

compression, lossy   160
> See *lossy compression*.

compression, LZW   159
> See *LZW compression*.

compression, MPEG   161
> See *MPEG*.

compression, runlength-encoding   159
> See *runlength encoding*.

concave   34
> A property of a polygon that has at least one vertex bulge inward instead of outward. See the text for a more rigorous definition.

curved patch   63

A primitive used to model a small piece, or patch, of a surface. A curved patch, as opposed to a polygon, can have edges that are not straight.

degauss   12

An action performed on a CRT monitor to demagnetize the CRT and any material near it. CRTs are very sensitive to external magnetic fields. Such fields can cause alignment, convergence, purity, and image-distortion problems. Most CRT monitors automatically perform degaussing when they are first switched on.

deflection yoke   8

Coils mounted on a CRT that are used to steer the electron beam.

depth buffer   96

See *Z buffer.*

depth-buffer rendering   96

See *Z-buffer rendering.*

The particular pattern of threshold values used in dithering. Some dither patterns are random, while others are applied as repeating tiles across the whole image.

A technique for increasing an image's apparent color (or grayscale) resolution without increasing the number of color (or gray) levels actually used, at the cost of adding a grainy look to the image.

A measure of how closely spaced the phosphor triads are on the face of a color CRT. The triads are arranged in a hexagonal pattern, and the dot pitch is the distance from the center of one triad to the center of any of its six neighbors. Dot pitch is usually specified in millimeters. Typical values are from .2 to .3 mm.

A mathematical operation of two vectors that produces a scalar. If both vectors have a length of 1 (unit vectors), then the dot product is the perpendicular projection of one vector onto the other.

The width of a point, or dot, primitive. Unlike mathematical points, computer graphics point primitives must have finite width to be visible. Many graphics subsystems allow the application to specify a width for such point primitives.

Dots per inch. This is a common measure of how close individual dots are on some output devices, such as inkjet printers.

Dynamic random-access memory. Most computer main memories are implemented with DRAM.

dye sublimation printer 21
See *printer, dye sublimation.*

electron gun 8
The part of a cathode-ray tube (CRT) that emits the electron beam.

emissive color 118
An object surface property sometimes used with the Phong lighting model. An object's emissive color is independent of any illumination. It therefore appears as if the object were emitting the color.

even field 17
See *field, even.*

exclusive OR 69
See *XOR operator.*

explicit surface modeling 62
A class of modeling techniques that define objects by providing an explicit list of patches that cover their surfaces. These surface patches can be either polygons or any of a number of curved surface patch types. Other modeling techniques work on volumes or only define an object's surface implicitly.

eye point 88
The point, or coordinate from which a scene is being viewed. This is also called the *camera point.*

eye ray 105
A ray in ray tracing that originates at the eye point. All recursively generated rays have an eye ray as their original ancestor.

eye vector 117
A vector from anywhere in the scene to the eye point. Eye vectors are usually unitized before use. The eye vector is needed in computing the apparent color when the object's surface properties include specular reflection.

facet shading 117
A shading method where the shading normal vector is taken from the geometric normal of the surface actually drawn. This makes the surface patches visible, especially if they are planar.

field   17

Half of a complete video frame when interlacing is used. The two
fields are referred to as the *odd* and the *even*. Each field contains
only every other scan line.

field, even   17

The first of the two fields that make up a frame in interlaced
video.

field, odd   17

The second of the two fields that make up a frame in interlaced
video.

film recorder   21

A computer output device that can write images to film.

filter, antialiasing, box   140

See *antialiasing filter, box*.

filter, antialiasing, good-quality   140

See *antialiasing filter, good-quality*.

filter, box   140

See *antialiasing filter, box*.

filter kernel   141

The function that defines the relative weight of a point depending
on its position. The relative weight is used in computing a
weighted average. This is actually a convolution operation, which is
commonly used in antialiasing.

filtering   140

This is a broad term that can mean the removal of coffee grinds
from the coffee. However, within the narrow usage of this book, a
filtering operation is the same as a convolution operation (see
convolution). Antialiasing is usually done by filtering.

flat projection   89

A method of projecting a 3D scene onto a 2D image such that the
resulting object sizes are not dependent on their position. Flat
projection can be useful when a constant scale is needed
throughout an image, such as in some mechanical drawings.

flat shading   126

A shading method where each pixel of a primitive is drawn with
the same color.

form factors 111

The name for the illumination coupling factors between polygons used in radiosity. Each form factor indicates how much light from one polygon will reach another polygon.

fractal 76

Something that has infinite detail. You will always see more detail as you magnify a small portion of a fractal. Mandelbrot set functions are examples of 2D fractals.

frame 17

One complete video image. When interlacing is used, a frame is composed of two fields, each containing only half the scan lines.

front end 22

The part of a display controller that receives drawing commands from the processor and writes the primitives into the bitmap.

gaze direction 88

The direction in which the virtual camera is pointed in the scene description. The center of the image will display whatever is along the gaze direction from the eye point.

geometric normal vector 116

A normal vector of the primitives as they are actually drawn. This often differs from the normal vector of the surface that was being modeled. Facet shading results when the shading normal vector is taken from the geometric normal vector.

GIF 165

A file format for storing images. GIF stands for Graphics Interchange Format and is owned by CompuServe, Incorporated.

Gouraud shading 127

See *interpolation, bilinear*.

graftal 77

A modeling technique where complex shapes are defined as relatively simple, recursive procedures.

graphic primitive 31

An object that the graphics system is capable of drawing into the bitmap. Examples are lines, points, and some polygons.

graphics card 22

See *display controller*.

interpolation 125

The mathematical process of determining plausible in-between values, given explicit values at particular points. Pixel values of polygons are often interpolated from values explicitly calculated at the vertices. Interpolation is usually much faster than explicitly calculating values.

inverse dynamics 154

A method for specifying motion in an animation. Linkages and other constraints are defined for the objects. A final state is then specified for some of the objects, and the computer calculates the motion of all the objects so that the final state is reached. Unlike in inverse kinematics, dynamic properties are taken into account, such as momentum, friction, and energy loss in collisions.

inverse kinematics 154

A method for specifying motion in an animation. Linkages and other constraints are defined for the objects. A final state is then specified for some of the objects, and the computer calculates the motion of all the objects so that the final state is reached.

isosurface 65

An implicit surface that exists wherever a continuous scalar field in a volume is at a particular value (the isovalue).

interpolation, bilinear 127

See *bilinear interpolation*.

INTERSECTION operator 68

See *AND operator*.

jaggies 138

See *aliasing*.

Java 165

A platform-independent way of defining procedures for use with World Wide Web documents.

JPEG 161

A lossy image file compression technique for still images.

key frame 152

A selected frame of an animation at which all the scene state is defined. In the key-frame animation method, the scene state at key

light vector 122

A vector from a point on an object toward a light source. Light vectors are usually unitized before use. A light vector is needed for each light source in computing the apparent color when the object's surface properties include diffuse or specular reflection.

linear interpolation 127

Interpolation is the process of determining plausible in-between values, given explicit values at particular points. Linear means that the values fall along a line from one known point to the next. This means the value changes a fixed amount for a fixed-sized step. Sometimes the term linear interpolation is used to refer to *bilinear interpolation*.

linear shading 127

See *bilinear interpolation*.

logical operator 68

See *Boolean operator*.

lookat point 89

A point in the scene that will project to the center of the image. The gaze vector points from the eye point toward a lookat point.

lossless compression 158

A compression scheme (see *compression*) where all data is preserved. The data may be compressed and decompressed any number of times without causing any changes. The compression ratio of lossless compression schemes is generally lower than that of lossy schemes. Runlength and LZW encoding are examples of lossless compression schemes.

lossy compression 160

A compression scheme (see *compression*) where some data may be irreversibly lost in favor of a high compression ratio. Many lossy schemes can trade off between amount of loss and the compression ratio. JPEG and MPEG are examples of lossy compression schemes for images.

lookup table 25

See *color lookup table*.

LUT 25

See *color lookup table*.

LZW compression 159

A digital data-compression scheme that works by identifying and compressing recurring patterns in the data. LZW stands for Lempel-Ziv and Welch. Unisys Corporation now claims that LZW compression is covered by its U.S. patent number 4,558,302.

Mach bands 131

An optical illusion caused by a sudden change in the rate of change of the brightness (discontinuities in the brightness' second derivative). This can give the appearance of a light or dark line at the sudden change.

Mandelbrot set 76

A popular mathematical function that exhibits fractal characteristics.

material properties 118

See *surface properties*.

MINUS operator 69

A constructive solid geometry (CSG) modeling operation on two objects. For the operation "*a* MINUS *b*," the resulting object exists wherever *A* existed without being coincident with *B*. This operation can also be expressed "*a* AND (NOT *b*)."

modeling 61

As used in this book, the process of creating a description of an object or scene for the purpose of subsequent rendering.

modeling, explicit surface 62

See *explicit surface modeling*.

modeling, implicit surface 65

See *implicit surface modeling*.

modeling, level of detail 79

modeling, polygon 62

See *polygon modeling*.

modeling, potential functions 67

See *potential function*.

modeling, procedural 76

See *procedural modeling*.

modeling, space subdivision 69

See *space subdivision modeling*.

OpenGL 166

A 3D graphics procedural interface. It was developed by Silicon Graphics, Incorporated, based on its earlier proprietary GL graphics library.

OR operator 68

A constructive solid geometry (CSG) modeling operator on two objects. The resulting object exists where either or both input objects exist. This operation is also called UNION.

origin 49

The point in a coordinate space where all coordinates are zero.

orthographic projection 91

See *flat projection*.

overlay where not zero 133

A simple image-compositing method where the overlay image results wherever it's not 0, and the background image results wherever the overlay image is 0. This method is rather simplistic, but it is sometimes supported in low-end hardware. It can be useful in overlaying text, for example. Alpha buffering is a more general compositing method.

palette image format 157

A format for storing an image that works much like pseudo color in a display controller. Each pixel contains a color ID instead of the actual color value. The true color represented by each color ID is defined in a table called the *palette*, which must also be stored with the image. A palette is much like a LUT in a pseudo color display controller.

parametric animation 153

An animation control method where scene state is determined by mathematical functions or computer procedures that take animation time as an input parameter.

particle system 78

A modeling technique where objects are defined by the collective tracks of many individual particles. Randomness is usually used to determine the details for each particle automatically, although overall guidance is supplied by the user.

persistence of vision 9

The property of the human visual system to continue seeing an image a short time (fraction of a second) after the image has gone away.

perspective projection 89

A method of projecting a 3D scene onto a 2D image such that distant objects are displayed smaller than near ones. A normal camera produces images using perspective projection.

Phong lighting model 115

A particular method for computing the apparent color of an object at a particular point.

Phong shading 127

A shading method where the shading normal vector is interpolated for each pixel, then used in a separate apparent color calculation for that pixel.

phosphor (or phosphors) 8

The material coating the inside of a CRT face. Phosphors have the special property that they emit light when struck by an electron beam.

phosphor persistence 10

The property of phosphors to stay lit a short time (fraction of a second) after the electron beam is cut off or moved away.

phosphor triad 10

One red, green, and blue phosphor dot on the face of a color CRT. The dots are arranged in an equilateral triangle. Triads are arranged in a hexagonal pattern, such that each triad is the same distance from each of its six neighbors.

pixel 1

The smallest indivisible unit of a digital image. A pixel is always the same color throughout. An image is a two-dimensional array of pixels.

point light source 87

A light source where all the light comes from one point. Although real light gets dimmer farther from a light source, a computer graphics point light source shouldn't be assumed to work that way unless explicitly stated.

printer, dye sublimation 21

A type of printer that works by evaporating controlled amounts of dye from a ribbon onto the page. The amount of dye can be accurately controlled, yielding continuous color resolution. Dye sublimation printers are relatively expensive, but they produce output comparable in quality to the traditional, wet-silver photographic process.

printer, inkjet 20

A type of printer that shoots tiny droplets of ink onto the page. Inkjet printers are a relatively low cost way to get computer graphics output.

printer, laser 20

A type of printer that works almost like a photocopier. The image is created by a laser under computer control, instead of coming from an original document as in a photocopier.

printer, thermal wax 20

See *printer, wax transfer*.

printer, wax transfer 20

A type of printer that works by depositing small specks of wax from a ribbon onto the page. The ribbon is pressed against the page, and wax is transferred wherever the ribbon is heated. This type of printer is also called *thermal wax*.

procedural model 76

An object model defined implicitly by a procedure that can produce volume or surface elements.

projection, flat 89

See *flat projection*.

projection method 89

A scheme for mapping the 3D scene geometry onto the 2D image.

projection, orthographic 89

See *flat projection*.

projection, perspective 89

See *perspective projection*.

pseudo-color system 25

A graphics system that stores pseudo colors, instead of true colors, in its bitmap. Pseudo colors are translated to true colors by the color lookup table (LUT).

bounding volume is maintained for each group in the hierarchy. If a ray doesn't intersect a bounding volume, then it definitely doesn't intersect any subordinate object in the hierarchy.

ray tracing, space subdivision 108

A ray-tracing speedup method where the scene space is subdivided into blocks. A list is kept for each block indicating which objects a ray could hit in that block. As a ray is traced, it is walked through the blocks, checking for intersection only with the objects listed in each block.

ray-tracing speed issues 104

recursive ray tracing 101

See *ray tracing.*

reflection vector 120

A vector used in the Phong lighting model to compute the specular reflection. It is usually unitized and points in the direction light is reflecting off the object.

refresh rate 16

The rate at which parts of the image on a CRT are repainted, or refreshed. The *horizontal refresh rate* is the rate at which individual scan lines are drawn. The *vertical refresh rate* is the rate at which fields are drawn in interlaced mode, or whole frames are drawn in noninterlaced mode.

refresh rate, horizontal 16

The rate at which scan lines are drawn when the image on a CRT is redrawn, or refreshed.

refresh rate, vertical 16

The rate at which fields are redrawn on a CRT when in interlaced mode, or the rate at which the whole image is redrawn when in noninterlaced mode.

regular BSP tree 75

See *BSP tree, regular.*

rendering 93

The process of deriving a 2D image from the 3D scene description. This is basically the "drawing" step.

resolution 1

The measure of how closely spaced the pixels are in a displayed image. For example, if 1,024 pixels are displayed across a screen that is 12 inches wide, then the image has a resolution of 85 pixels per inch.

RGB 3

A color space where colors are defined as mixtures of the three additive primary colors red, green, and blue.

right vector 89

A vector sometimes used to define the virtual camera orientation in a scene description. This is more typically done with an up vector.

runlength encoding 159

A lossless digital-data-compression scheme. It identifies identical consecutive values and replaces them with just one copy of the value and a repeat count.

scalar 40

A regular, single number, as opposed to a vector.

scan line 157

One line in a raster scan. Also used to mean one horizontal row of pixels.

scan-line order 157

A way of arranging image data so that all the pixels for one scan line are stored or transmitted before the pixels for the next scan line.

scan rate 16

See *refresh rate*.

scattered light 111

See *secondary scatter*.

scene 83

The complete 3D description of everything needed to render an image. This includes all the object models, the light sources, and the viewing geometry.

secondary scatter 111

Light that is reflected from a nonemitting object that illuminates other objects. This is the kind of interobject illumination that is computed by radiosity.

shading 113

This term is used several ways in computer graphics. However, shading always has something to do with figuring out pixel color values, as opposed to figuring out the geometry or which pixels are to be drawn.

shading, bilinear   127

See *bilinear interpolation*.

shading, facet   117

See *facet shading*.

shading, flat   126

See *flat shading*.

shading, Gouraud   127

See *bilinear interpolation*.

shading, linear   127

See *bilinear interpolation*.

shading normal vector   116

The normal vector used in determining the apparent color of an object. In facet shading, the shading normal is the geometric normal of the primitives used to model the surface. In smooth shading, the shading normal is the normal vector of the surface that was modeled. The shading normal vector may be further modified by bump mapping.

shadow mask   10

A thin layer in a color CRT that the electron beams cannot penetrate. It is suspended just in front of (from the electron beam's point of view) the phosphor screen. The shadow mask has one hole for each phosphor color triad. Due to the position of the phosphor triads, the shadow mask holes, and the angle of the three electron beams, each electron beam can hit only the phosphor dots of its assigned color.

SIGGRAPH   164

The Special Interest Group on Graphics of the Association for Computing Machinery (ACM). SIGGRAPH is the premier professional association for computer graphics.

smooth shading   117

Any shading technique that attempts to make the rendered surface appear more like what was modeled instead of like the primitives used to approximate that model. This is usually done by taking the shading normal vector from the modeled surface instead of from the geometric normal vector.

See *3D texture*.

See *adaptive space subdivision*.

A modeling technique where the scene is broken into small regions of space. A list of the objects present is kept for each region. Examples of space subdivision modeling are BSP trees and octrees.

See *ray tracing, space subdivision*.

The color of an object's shiny highlights. Specular reflection also depends on the specular exponent. Both these parameters are part of the object's surface properties.

This is a scalar value that controls the "tightness" of the specular highlights. A value of 0 causes the specular color to be reflected equally in all directions, just like the diffuse color. An infinite value causes it to be reflected the same way a mirror would. Common values are about 5 to 60.

See *B-spline*.

See *beta spline*.

A curved surface that takes its shape from the placement of a set of control points.

A light source that does not shine in all directions, but is usually directed in a cone shape. This is a convenient hack for modeling lamps with shades or reflectors, without actually having to compute the effect of the shade or reflector during rendering.

An input pixel to an operation that uses multiple smaller pixels at higher resolution to compute each resulting pixel at the final resolution. This is done, for example, in an antialiasing filtering operation.

surface orientation, apparent 117

See *apparent surface orientation.*

surface properties 118

The collective name for all the object-specific parameters that are used to compute the apparent color of a point on that object. These include the diffuse color, specular color, and so forth. The term *surface properties* is common but not standard. Other names for the same thing are *visual properties*, or *material properties*.

temporal aliasing 142

Aliasing in time by animation frame instead of spatially by pixel. The visual effect of temporal aliasing has been called *strobing*. Moving objects appear to jump through a sequence of frozen steps instead of in smooth paths.

tessellation level 62

The relative fineness or granularity of the patches used to model a surface. A model with smaller, and therefore more, patches is said to have a higher tessellation level.

tessellation 62

The act of tiling a surface with individual surface patches.

texil 143

One pixel of a texture map, where the texture map is an image. In diffuse color texture mapping, the texture value is a color. The texture color values are therefore often supplied as an image. A texil is one pixel of this image, as opposed to one pixel of the final image being rendered.

texture, 3D 146

See *3D texture.*

texture map 143

The external function that supplies the texture value in texture mapping. In diffuse color texture mapping, the texture map is a set of color values in two dimensions. This is usually specified as an image. Note, however, that not all texture maps are images, because not all textures are two-dimensional color values. Bump mapping is a form of texture mapping where the texture is not an image because the texture values are shading normal vector perturbations instead of colors.

texture mapping 143

The process where some parameter of the apparent color computation is replaced by an external function, called the *texture map*. A common example is texture-mapping an object's diffuse color from an image. This gives the appearance of the image painted onto the object. Bump mapping is another form of texture mapping discussed in this book.

texture mapping, diffuse color 143

A form of texture mapping where the texture defines the object's diffuse color. This gives the appearance of pasting the texture image onto the object.

texture mapping, normal vector perturbations 146

See *bump mapping*.

thermal wax printer 20

See *printer, wax transfer*.

TIFF 165

Tag Image File Format. A common image file format. Just about all applications that can import image files support the TIFF format.

toner 20

The material that is deposited onto the page to form the image in a photocopier or laser printer.

transform, 3D 48

See *3D transform*.

transformation matrix, 3D 53

See *3D transform*.

transparency value 133

See *alpha value*.

triad 10

See *phosphor triad*.

triangle strip primitive 38

A graphic primitive that contains a set of successively abutting triangles. A triangle strip primitive is more efficient than the equivalent separate triangle primitives. It is also called a *Tstrip*.

    An operation between a vector and a scalar. The resulting vector is the same as the input vector, except that its magnitude (length) is multiplied by the scalar. Scaling a vector by the reciprocal of its magnitude results in a unit vector.

    The width of a vector, or line segment, primitive. Unlike mathematical line segments, computer graphics vector primitives must have a finite width to be visible. Many graphics systems allow the application to specify a width for such primitives.

    The part of a display controller that reads the pixel data in the bitmap and produces the live video signals. Among other components, the back end contains the color lookup tables (LUTs), the digital-to-analog converters (DACs), and the logic to generate the video timing signals.

virtual reality 19

A name loosely applied to systems that attempt to immerse the user in a virtual world generated by the computer. This is often done with a stereoscopic display that is updated based on head position and usually includes some sort of 3D pointing device. More advanced systems include 3D sound and some form of touch feedback. This is still a rapidly changing area.

visual properties 118

See *surface properties*.

voxel 72

A unit of subdivided space. Voxel stands for *volume element*. Nodes in an octree, for example, are referred to as voxels.

VRAM 28

Video random-access memory. This is really DRAM with additional features specifically for use as bitmap memory in display controllers. VRAM typically costs twice as much as DRAM, but it allows the drawing engine full access to the bitmap, independently from the video back end. This can increase the hardware drawing rate.

VRML 165

Virtual Reality Modeling Language. The standard description language for 3D graphics in World Wide Web documents.

wax transfer printer 20

See *printer, wax transfer*.

Web browser 165

Software that can read and display World Wide Web documents.

wire frame 93

A rendering method where only the outlines of objects and primitives are drawn.

World Wide Web 164

A set of interconnected documents on the Internet that adhere to the HTML standard. The World Wide Web is often abbreviated as WWW.

WWW 164

See *World Wide Web*.

XOR operator 69

A constructive solid geometry (CSG) modeling operation on two objects. The resulting object exists where each object existed alone, not coincident with each other. XOR is an abbreviation for "exclusive or."

X Windows   166

A window management and 2D graphics environment that is very common on Unix systems.

Z buffer   96

The collective name for all the Z values in a bitmap.

Z-buffer rendering   96

A rendering method where an additional depth, or Z, value is kept per pixel. A pixel is overwritten by a new primitive only if the new Z value represents a shorter distance, or depth, from the eye point. The end result is an image of the frontmost surface of the front-most objects.

Z value   96

The name for the value that represents distance from the eye point in a Z-buffer rendering system.